HELEN'S
African
Journey

a 1934 visit

Judith G. duPont

Printed in the United States of America
ISBN 978-1-956019-64-3 (Paperback)
ISBN 978-1-956019-65-0 (ebook)

Canoe Tree
Press
4697 Main Street
Manchester Center, VT 05255
Canoe Tree Press is a division of DartFrog Books

Preface

My mother had always told my brothers and me that she had traveled to Africa. We understood that she had gone alone, when she was Helen Odell, before being married to our father. Her stories about the primitive amenities out in the bush amused us, and we liked to examine some tiny ivory animals she brought back. But that was the extent of it. Only after she died in 1979 did I find her diaries stacked neatly in the bottom drawer of her desk. Later I came across an embossed leather photo album filled with pictures of her 1934 trip as well as other clippings. Going through file boxes of papers, I discovered the letters she wrote to her mother and sister, plus a few sheets of manuscript about the trip. At one point she must have begun writing up her trip, but unfortunately stopped after describing the first week on the ship to Africa. The trip wasn't a secret. It just belonged to the past. Her life had become dedicated to her husband and children plus an array of other projects and interests. However, she had carefully saved the Africa material, understanding that someday it would tell her story.

How do we know what our parents were like before they were married, before we came along? As children, we never think about such things. Our parents loom large in our world, their personalities tied together in a package, wrapped around their care for us. But, of course, they did have earlier lives.

Uncovering a parent's past can introduce a curious new relative, unquestionably familiar but oddly unconnected to us. This is the person I got to know as I delved into my mother's long journey. She had the charm and sense of fun that I recognized but also sparks of obstinacy and rebelliousness that were quite surprising.

Once I began transcribing her 1934 diary and her letters home, I became increasingly interested in Africa, especially Southern Rhodesia, now Zimbabwe, and South Africa. In 1994 I went on a typical tour to Kenya and Tanzania, purposely selecting a two-day add-on to see Victoria Falls from the Zimbabwe side. While overnighting in Harare, I found a phone number for the name of my mother's friends in Bulawayo and called. A young man answered but had no idea what to tell me. After returning home, I wrote a letter explaining why I had called but then never received a reply; my questions went unanswered. Later I would discover that her friends never had any children, so most likely I had only reached distant relatives. A South Africa tour in 2011 was more successful. At least I could find some of the places my mother visited, take photos of my own, and get a hint of what it all might have been like almost eighty years earlier. But the African continent is a very different place today than it was during the last phase of the colonial period. The countries that my mother visited, that I visited, have been fighting for decades to destroy all traces of their colonial past. The history is painful and heartbreaking. Thus, finding people and places prominent in the 1930s can be almost impossible, and understandably so. The social and political perspectives have changed entirely.

Helen – let's call her by her first name as she wasn't anyone's mother in 1934 – was an inveterate traveler. But travel at that time seems practically unrecognizable to us, so in touch as we are to the world at our fingertips. Perhaps the most striking difference is the amount of time that was given over to transportation and especially to leisure trips. Her journey lasted over five months. She took three ocean liners and several trains just to visit an acquaintance and return home. Without the advantages of modern communication, travelers, like Helen, felt even further removed, if not completely disconnected from their normal existence. Spending weeks on luxury liners and in comfortable hotels with a social circle of total strangers created an alluring fictive world, easy to step into but sometimes not so easy to leave behind. The thought seemed to be why rush through these experiences or skip them altogether as we usually do today.

This story of a woman journeying alone to distant places echoes several other women's travel tales, but Helen was no Isabella Bird or Gertrude Bell. She was simply determined to discover whatever she could and, above all, enjoy herself. Coming of age in the 1920s, she saw herself as a "new woman," comfortable with her own independence. Many of her women friends traditionally waited at home for their lives to unfold in the customary ways. But, since that tactic wasn't leading her anywhere, why not travel to an interesting destination, actively go out into the world and perhaps create a unique future. In any event, Helen had no qualms about traveling, even alone.

CHAPTER ONE

Leaving

Have you ever wanted to leave home, just get out of town, take yourself somewhere completely different, and open up your life to new experiences? That is precisely what my mother must have wanted to do when she traveled to Africa in 1934. Single, she had recently turned 32 years old, and her life was spinning away in an endless round of luncheons, teas, golf and tennis games, cocktail parties, bridge games, and dinner parties. Wasn't there something else more interesting? Although she had tried to create an exciting new future for herself, by the end of 1933 the pattern was always the same. Was there a way to break that pattern and redesign her life? Perhaps she could pull travel out of her hat. It was not a new trick. It was one that had served her well in the past. Maybe this time an exotic trip would work just the right bit of magic.

My mother, Helen Odell, had been living at home for thirteen years ever since she dropped out of Smith College in the middle of her sophomore year. All those women together in Northampton, Massachusetts, just wasn't for her, she explained to me later. Initially, the plan was for her to transfer to Barnard College in New York, but somehow that never happened. Home for Helen, at first, was in Wilmington, Delaware, where her father Joseph Odell, a retired Presbyterian minister, directed the Service Citizens, a non-profit organization chiefly devoted to improving public education. She did make a couple of attempts to work in New York City, and she traveled, spending six months in Paris one winter. However, after her father's death from heart disease in 1929, Helen and her mother made their recently renovated summer house along the Connecticut shore in Stonington their permanent home.

By the time Helen had reached her thirties, she was finding it harder to shed an "old maid" stigma. She had always been popular and outgoing with plenty of friends. She was tall, five feet ten inches, and athletic, with light brown hair and pale blue eyes, not beautiful but immediately engaging thanks to her amiable personality and lively sense of fun. But now, most of her friends were married, and many had children. They had roles in life and work to do. Helen's role was that of a dutiful daughter and attractive single woman. It wasn't that she didn't have beaux, as boyfriends were called in those days. She had several. She'd also had several who just faded away, and now one who was happy to keep taking her out, seemingly indefinitely. This relationship was approaching a three-year anniversary. Would life go on this way forever?

When Helen announced her decision to go to Africa, her friends were stunned. She wrote later: "It was utterly appalling to me the lack of knowledge in America on the subject of Africa and the awe and interest aroused by the mere mention of my intended visit. If I had said that I intended to fly the Atlantic alone, it would not have caused more wonderment to my friends than this proposed trip by myself. That I would die of fever, be eaten by a lion, be abducted by natives, or marry a ne'er-do-well were all expected by one or another."

It sounds as though Helen's friends had little confidence in her daring. This quite sensible single woman was proposing to do something extraordinary, something that might not end well. Less than two years earlier Amelia Earhart had successfully flown the Atlantic alone. Helen's solo adventure seemed to have poorer odds. And, why Africa? Was Helen interested in joining people like Ernest Hemingway on safari in Tanganyika? She might not have even been aware of the newly popular writer, and although she had done some duck hunting, big game was not her quarry. No apparent interest there. But Africa was a completely unique and fascinating destination. And, with a friend living there, the possibilities for having a very good time beckoned.

Helen would be leaving her mother, Winifred Odell, and their comfortable house and English-style garden in Stonington, leaving those skeptical friends and leaving those endless social engagements. She would also be leaving her attractive young beau who enjoyed her company but avoided discussing plans for the future. Never mind. Her love of travel and new adventures as well as her desire to shape her own future pushed her onward. After all, she would be back in a few months, the date not exactly certain as she did not book any return passage.

Helen's home in Stonington (author collection)

Helen really did have a friend living in Africa, an English girl, Lorna Keilor, who had married a young man named Robert Tredgold in 1925 and gone to live in Bulawayo, Southern Rhodesia. Lorna had written from time to time encouraging Helen to visit, but did she realize what such a trip would entail? Did she ever dream that Helen would actually come? Dropping into Bulawayo wasn't exactly like visiting the Loire chateaus from Paris, which Helen had done handily in 1929. Trans-Atlantic airline passenger service was about five years off, to say nothing of service to and from Africa. Helen's trip would have to be by ocean liner, in fact by two liners and a train in order to get from the coast of the Portuguese colony of Mozambique to landlocked Southern Rhodesia. This self-governing British colony had been originally claimed in the 1890s by Cecil Rhodes and his British South Africa Company as part of their quest for gold and diamonds. The country, which stretches between the Limpopo and Zambezi Rivers, finally achieved independence in 1980 and is now known as Zimbabwe. But, in the 1930s Southern Rhodesia was still finding its way between making peace with the Ndebele native peoples and establishing a functioning government and legal system. To put it simply, the colony was a frontier land, not a tourist destination.

Helen first met Lorna Keilor ten years earlier, in April of 1924, shortly after arriving at her Auntie Gertie's house in Buckland, a small village just north of Frome in Somerset, England. Both of Helen's parents were English and had immigrated to the United States after they were married in 1894, leaving their families behind. Helen had traveled to England several times with her mother, but when she reached her twenties, the Odells wanted their daughter to experience more of English life and really get to know her relatives. Living with Winifred's sister, Gertrude Standing, for several months could accomplish that, for a reasonable contribution toward room and board, of course.

Toward the end of 1923 Helen had taken an entry-level job in New York City at *The Spur*, a magazine covering sports for wealthy socialites, and she lived at the Allerton House on 57th Street, a building exclusively for business and professional women. However, it seems that the job at *The Spur* didn't provide enough challenge or money to support staying in the city. In January, John McKay, the president of *The Spur*, wrote to Joseph Odell, "We were all sorry to have lost Miss Odell from the office. She was doing most intelligent work and we were counting on passing on more important work later." (So typical, and when were they planning on telling Miss Odell about this work?) McKay goes on to say that he thought giving her the "opportunity" to visit relatives in England was "wise."

Winifred Odell's older sister Gertrude was a widow and lived in a 17th century stone house called "The Old Parsonage," next to St. Michael's Church in Buckland, where Lorna Keilor's father was the vicar. The two young women were introduced the day after Helen arrived. The following Saturday Helen wrote in her diary, "After dinner we went over to the Keilors' and talked and listened to the radio. Wouldn't I die of boredom if I had to live like this at home?" It's not surprising that the boredom, along with cold damp weather, got to the 22-year-old Helen. Her trans-Atlantic trip on the Royal Mail liner *Orca* had been a ten day "whirl," beginning with an onboard send-off party in New York, her friends bearing gifts of flowers, candy, books, perfume, as well as a carton of Lucky Strikes. She immediately joined a lively group of new friends on board and played bridge, deck golf, and deck tennis every day. The evenings usually started with cocktail parties in various people's cabins and ended up after dinner with friends drinking champagne, dancing, laughing, and having "a very jolly time" especially at the costume ball and the gala. By comparison, dinners alone with eccentric Auntie Gertie and evenings with the Keilor family must have seemed very slow.

Nevertheless, Lorna provided companionship for Helen and a break from Auntie Gertie's prickly personality, upsetting emotional outbreaks, and dull routine. As the summer got under way, tennis parties, sightseeing, and a rainy, muddy but "jolly" day trip to the Epsom Derby with Joseph Odell's brother Uncle Wal and his wife Auntie Maude, perked things up. But it was through Lorna that Helen became better friends with the "most attractive" Sylvia

Duckworth, whose family owned the nearby estate, Orchardleigh Manor. More tennis parties, picnics, and teas with the sophisticated gentry followed. In July Lorna went off to Dulverton in the western part of Somerset to work for the summer at a country inn, mostly picking fruit and arranging flowers. Helen, happy to break away from "The Old Parsonage" for a few weeks, followed as a paying guest. To her delight, the inn provided horseback riding and salmon fishing in the River Exe. She rode across the moors every day and helped Lorna around the stable yard and in the gardens. She even hired a car and driver for a day's tour of the *Lorna Doone* countryside. "I love it so, I can't tear myself away," Helen wrote home.

Lorna was planning to be married in the coming year. Her fiancé, Robert Clarkson Tredgold, was from an eminent colonial family. His father, Clarkson Tredgold, had been the Attorney-General of Rhodesia and currently served as Chief Justice in the capital Salisbury. His mother, Emily Ruth, was the niece of David Livingstone and the daughter of John Moffat, a missionary who in 1887 forged the first treaty with Lobengula, the tribal leader of Zambesia. Lorna and Robert had met in Richmond, England, when Robert would visit old friends of his father's during his vacations from Oxford University. Lorna had been taking care of the Lord Chancellor's garden on the grounds of the old Palace at Richmond. The two became engaged, and Robert, a Rhodes Scholar who studied law at Hertford College, Oxford, was called to the Bar by the Inner Temple early in 1923. He then returned to his birthplace, Bulawayo, Southern Rhodesia, to establish a law practice before marrying. The wedding was scheduled for the fall of 1925 in Cape Town, South Africa. In a letter from Dulverton, Helen wrote to her family, "Lorna Keilor is a knock-out. The more I see of her the more I love her. She wants me to come out and visit her in Rhodesia in a couple of years but it is rather a trip, to say the least. I wish she weren't going so far away."

Although Helen and Lorna became close friends that summer of 1924, enjoying the English country life together, their past experiences and future expectations were quite different. Their fathers were ministers, and both girls had given up on higher education, but there the similarities ended. Helen was well on her way to becoming a 1920s "modern woman." She wanted to be a writer and had spent time in New York. She found friends everywhere she went and loved parties and sports; combining the two activities was even better. With Auntie Gertie as a chaperone, Helen visited London several times during the summer where she ran into American friends including a fellow named Luther. One evening he took her to see the musical "Toni" and then on to a Mayfair nightclub. The Prince of Wales just happened to be at the theater and dropped in to the club as well. Lorna, on the other hand, stuck close to her family and was evidently serious about gardening and the outdoor life. Going off to live in Africa would be somewhat of an adjustment for her. More likely it would have been a greater adjustment for Helen. After "a typical vicarage tea" one afternoon at the Keilors' house, Helen wrote in her diary, "Lorna showed me her trousseau things. They are very well done but imagine an American girl getting married with things like that."

In September, after spending a lively two weeks in Paris with

American friends, Helen returned to Wilmington and her parents. She filled her days with volunteer work, her afternoons and evenings with social engagements. She joined the Junior League and was named the Wilmington president in 1927, but the following year found her packing again. Paris was *the* place to be for Americans looking for sophistication, culture, and excitement in the twenties, and Helen had devised a way to get back there. Beginning in October 1928 she lived with a family on the rue d'Assas overlooking the Luxembourg Gardens and worked part time for the University of Delaware junior year abroad program. She must have been so busy that keeping a diary was out of the question. Just snippets of letters and notes remain to prove that Helen made the most of her stay, taking French lessons, traveling around Europe, and having teas and dinners with politicians and minor nobility. Among her mementos are two photographs of her friend Fenza, the Countess Sobotka, and the guest list for a farewell tea party she gave. The list of about 30 women included Parisians and several American friends who happened to be staying in Paris, one being the opera singer Alice Tully. Only her father's struggle with worsening heart disease compelled Helen to leave Paris early and return home in May on the liner *Ile de France.*

Helen's life in Connecticut during the early thirties was pleasant enough, but it wasn't Paris. Having been very close to her father, she found it difficult to shake off the grief caused by his death, and she accompanied her mother back to England in December 1929 to spend the winter with family. But most of her time was spent in Stonington. According to her 1932 diary, days were filled with the usual golf and tennis as well as singing lessons, riding, and even hawk-shooting. Almost every evening she went out for cocktails (despite Prohibition being still in effect), dinner or entertained at home. She went to lots of movies with friends and frequently played card games like bridge, 21, and Michigan, even roulette. For a change of pace, she occasionally took the train to New York City for a few days of shopping, seeing friends, and going to the theater. Although Al, her steady beau in Stonington, usually showed up in the city to take her to dinner, she frequently juggled dates with him and new heart throbs on alternate evenings. However, Helen's diary entry for November 30, 1932 in New York was short and sweet, "Dinner with Al – nightclubs – gardenias…"

How Helen's life was progressing in 1933 is somewhat of a mystery as she left no diary for that year. Was there one, and did she decide to destroy it? We will never know. What we do know is that 1933 is generally what historians call the depth of the Depression, a year with very high unemployment and very low hope for recovery any time soon. With the severe stock market decline and bank failures, spending was curtailed, and couples postponed marrying, causing the marriage rate to dramatically decline. Just under twenty-five percent of all women were actually employed, a figure that included nurses, teachers, and domestics. Thus, Helen, who didn't marry early and who didn't have a career, faced an uncertain and possibly bleak future.

But the elegance of the twenties lingered for some; think Fred Astaire and Ginger Rogers dancing "The Carioca" in *Flying Down to Rio* or the smooth charm of Duke Ellington's "Sophisticated Lady." Perhaps the Depression was responsible for Al not proposing to

Helen, but clearly he was having too much fun enjoying the single life. Almost four years younger than Helen, he turned only twenty-eight in 1933. He had an executive sales job at his brother-in-law's manufacturing business in Mystic, Connecticut, but evenings, weekends, and short stays in New York provided plenty of time for diversion, from boating and horseback riding to partying, especially dancing with graceful women. By the fall of '33 Helen must have come to the conclusion that she really couldn't continue to wait around for a man to sweep her up. It would be up to her to make a break and, incidentally, demonstrate some astonishing independence.

Without a 1933 diary or letters, we miss out on what Helen went through to arrange her trip. There must have been letters back and forth with Lorna, each one surely taking at least a month to reach its destination. Somehow passage on a ship from England to Africa was secured, perhaps with the help of the venerable travel agency, Thomas Cook & Son. That in turn required passage from New York to Southampton, and the decision was made to team up with another girl from the Stonington area who was going to visit friends in England. A hotel was booked to allow for a two week stay in London before the Africa voyage. And then there was the packing. How should one pack for London in January, formal evenings on ocean liners, and months of Africa's sweltering heat? In nine pieces of luggage, of course. Keep in mind that this was the 1930s, and the world was better arranged for heavily burdened travelers.

On Monday, January 1, 1934, Helen started right off recording a busy New Years' Day in her red National Diary. Packing notwithstanding, she went off to an afternoon cocktail party ("great fun") and later, after dinner, to play bridge until midnight. The next day she took her trunk to the railroad station to check it, probably on the UPS-precursor Railway Express, straight through to the pier in New York. (That might have been the large, well-worn wardrobe trunk with hangers and drawers that I used to marvel at in my grandmother's attic). At last, on Wednesday, the day arrived to leave Stonington and drive to New York with a friend. The trip from the eastern end of Connecticut to the city took about five hours in those days, and it was far simpler to bring eight pieces of luggage by car. Happily, Al was in the city to escort her to cocktails, a late dinner at the Bijou restaurant, and dancing at the chic Central Park Casino near Fifth Avenue and 72nd Street (torn down in 1935). Helen wrote, "Had a grand time. Back to hotel. Al – too sweet." Another day in New York was filled with errands, getting a permanent wave at the hairdresser, and meeting up with her mother and several friends. Dinner and dancing at the Essex House until 2:20 A.M. did not include Al, "but all fixed in a long telephone call."

Finally, on Friday afternoon, January 5, after saying good-by to her mother, Helen boarded the elegant Cunard liner RMS *Mauretania*. (This *Mauretania*, launched in 1907, was retired later in 1934 and was replaced by a new *Mauretania* in 1938.) Thirteen friends came along with her for a proper *bon voyage* party, and traveling companion Kate Virginia Cottrell and her family joined them. "Great send off," Helen wrote in the diary, "I in tears when Al left at 5." But the whole event suffered an anticlimax when the ship had to postpone sailing due to thick fog and sat at the pier all night. In a last minute letter to her mother at 9:00 P.M., Helen described the ship:

My cabin is very nice & comfortable with two windows. The ship is empty. I am enclosing the [First Class] passenger list so you can see how few we are – mostly English people I believe, and business men, but of course I haven't had much chance as yet to look them over. Kavie and I have a table alone. Dinner was very good and the steward sweet but he forgot our soup. We gently & kindly called attention to it, and he was so chagrined, "Oh, Madame," he said, "such a deplorable lack of concentration." If you repeat that with the British accent, it makes a pretty good line.

I am not exaggerating when I say that I have at least 30 books, 15 boxes of flowers, gardenias, orchids & cut flowers; a pile of telegrams, roughly 17 letters; one potted plant; one huge tin of fresh caviar. Never have I seen such a display and the letters to be written are almost finishing me off, just to think of it. The steward & stewardess said that no one, not even any movie queens, ever in the life of the ship got so many packages. The purser, dining stewards, everyone calls us by name now as we are apparently famed & considered extraordinarily important.

Darling, I do hope you are not too tired and not blue on the eve of your daughter's departure. It seems so silly that I am now right here in New York, and so are you. I shall miss you and think you are the swellest mother a girl ever, ever had. All my love and thoughts are with you.

The *Mauretania*, which had held the trans-Atlantic speed record, delivered Helen and Kavie to Southampton, England in six days. Helen was able to get another letter off to her mother by mailboat on January 11. Rather than living alone all winter in Stonington, Winifred Odell had arranged to stay at the Drake Hotel in Philadelphia, near her sister Fanny, who lived in Swarthmore with her family, and Helen's older sister Marjorie in Wilmington, Delaware. Despite these plans, Helen worried about her mother being lonely.

Helen's mother, Winifred Odell (author collection)

Thurs, Jan. 11
Mother dear,

Well, the first lap of my trip is nearly over, I am sorry to say. We got to Plymouth this evening, and to Southampton tomorrow noon at which place we disembark. It has seemed so short, and certainly proves that there is a great difference between the small & large ships.

We have had lovely weather in that the sun has been shining every day until today, and warm enough to wear a suit on deck without a topcoat even, but even so it has been extraordinarily rough – even rougher I believe than that time on the [Cunard RMS] Ausonia. *Everything lashed down, ropes stretched on deck to hold on to. Nothing will stay on the table in the dining room, and several people have been hurled out of their chairs, one man hurt. I woke up this A.M. to find a gale blowing, and thunder & lightning but still warm & still rough. They are worrying about landing people at Plymouth, but I don't know of anyone who wants to get off there, and wonder why they stop.*

We have had an awfully pleasant time. We know a man named John Woodrough, aged 30, Hill [School] *& Princeton, who is going to England to live; starting in a business making & selling shaving cream & is settling in Peterborough. He's awfully nice – looks something like M– B– but is much nicer & much more fun & very generous. He had his deck chair put next to us & we have cocktails together in the evening & have been playing '21' at nights. It has been too rough to dance since the first night. … Also an elderly gentleman has won our hearts, mine especially & he is Mr. Hiltman, the president of Appleton's, the publisher. Of course he knows John Macrae* [Joseph Odell's editor at Dutton] *very well & others amongst our friends. He is sweet, & has the most marvelous sense of humour. He goes over every year and has stayed for 30 years at the Berkeley* [Hotel]. *Then there is a Mr. Chilton en route to China, and a Mr. Williams who is on his way to Salisbury,*

Rhodesia which is only 300 miles from Bulawayo. He is going to fly out from England. He is a Virginian, in the tobacco business there – has been there for years & has just been home on a visit. He is about 35 or so, fat & lazy, at least he acts half asleep all the time, but I guess it's just his Virginian manner. He tells me the train from Beira to Bulawayo only goes twice a week, but it is arranged to fit the ships so I guess I won't have to wait. He also says that I go through Salisbury & am there about 4 hours & he will meet me & take me around & put me back on the train. "Woodie" (John Woodrough) says he will come down from Peterborough & see me off in London and on the Llangibby Castle [the Union Castle liner for the London-Africa leg of the trip] *& will send me postcards & a radio or two on my way out. So, if all works out I should not feel too solitary on my long trip.*

Other passengers are a marvelous, typical English family with 4 children – fine type & awfully nice; Sir John Hewett, a big shot apparently in radio, & his daughter, Mrs. Atkinson – typical 'county;' and many business men, some very nice. There aren't more than 50 of us I find now in the 1st Class. There are about 50 I believe in Tourist. I have been down there a couple of times & how people can rave about it I don't see.

I have started smoking English cigarettes to save money & as yet, have not enjoyed them but hope to in time.

Mr. Williams does nothing but tell me how expensive everything is in Africa which is cheering.

Kavie is enjoying the trip as much as I, & is a grand girl. I like her tremendously, and she is the nicest person to travel with and is lots of fun.

I do wonder so much how you are getting o~~~~ (I just fell flat on the floor). It is terribly rough. Am so anxious to hear what you are doing. Please take good care of yourself. I miss you & our nice talks. Have a good time.

Much, much love,
Helen

Apparently neither afraid nor seasick, Helen and Kavie seemed to have made the most of a dreary Atlantic crossing. With only 57 passengers in First Class, the ship indeed must have been very empty, as the normal First Class capacity was several hundred, but between the Depression and the January weather, it wouldn't have been surprising. Helen's rather snobby comments about Tourist Class are a little puzzling, but might be expected from someone who had made eight trans-Atlantic round trip crossings, always in First Class. Even a traditional Gala Dinner never happened, making it a very subdued voyage indeed. Still, Helen managed to make new friends, including Mr. Williams, who filled her in on some crucial details having to do with her Rhodesia arrangements. It is surprising that she did not realize that the train followed the liners' schedules, and she would not have to spend a few nights in Beira, Mozambique all alone.

Once she arrived in London and checked into the hotel in Mayfair, Helen got to work contacting relatives, old friends, and people she had been urged to look up. She also picked up mail, and presumably money, at the merchant bank Brown Shipley, which she and her family had used often in the past. The Thomas

Cook & Son travel agency was handling her arrangements, and she managed to check in with them on Saturday morning as well. But it is her social adventures in London that are well told in letters to her mother.

Fleming's New Clarges Hotel
Half Moon Street, Piccadilly,
London, W.1.
Sunday, Jan. 14th
Dearest Mother,

It was so rough that we never did stop at Plymouth, but we landed at Southampton at one o'clock on Friday. I had no trouble at all with the customs, and the sun was shining, and it was warm – almost like a nice April day. Everybody had a very jolly time in the train but I enjoyed looking out of the window and was surprised at the kick I got out of seeing England again. It really gave me a big thrill, also driving from Waterloo and seeing Westminster & all the other well-known sights through the late afternoon mist. Kavie & I have a nice double room here on the 1st floor, so it's noisy & we haven't slept very well. When we got in we lit the fire & had tea & it was very pleasant. Woodie however decided to stay over a few days in London & he came to this hotel too. He got tickets for Friday night for Beatrice Lillie in "Please." We dressed & dined & went to the Berkeley & danced. There was an Englishman at the table next to us alone. We picked him up & he joined us & later he took us to a club of his where we had coffee & eggs & danced some more. It was all great fun. But Woodie

has become a great problem. He should go on to Peterborough &
get to work, and he drinks all the time incessantly. He wasn't that
way on the ship but since he landed here he has been at it. We are
sick of it, & always uneasy that he will get too tight & embarrass
us & he bores us & we think he is just a lazy, weak, no-good sort
of boy. Last night we went to see "Nymph Errant" with Gertrude
Lawrence in it. We refused to go anywhere afterwards & we lit
in to him & told him he was starting out all wrong on his career
here, & that he was well on his way to becoming a dipsomaniac,
etc., etc. This morning he told us on the phone that he went out
alone when we came to bed & was out all night. We have refused
to see him today in the hopes that he will leave.

Having landed Friday afternoon, there wasn't much chance
to do things Saturday before 12 o'clock closing time & we could
write notes to people but they won't get them until tomorrow. No
one seems to have a phone. I did get hold of one Mr. & Mrs.
Nelson, friends of Kittsie Winfield's & am going there to tea this
afternoon. I have written to K. Mason & various other people.
Last night I sent Uncle Charlie a telegram at his old address as I
haven't got his new one, or Hilda & Arthur's. I said I'd like to go
out there today for the day & to ring me up here. But he never got
the wire. I rang up an A.S. Wright at Palmer's Green but it was
the wrong one & he didn't know Arthur or Uncle Charlie. I had
to give it up. I must now go & take the bus to St. John's Wood to
the Nelson's. I'll probably get lost but am determined not to take a
taxi. Will continue later.

Tuesday – 3 P.M.

Uncle Charlie & Auntie Gertie have just left, after having had lunch with me here. The telegram finally tracked him down yesterday & he rang me up. They wanted me to go out there but I simply couldn't – no time & I am indisposed & all. We had a nice lunch. Kavie was alone so had lunch with us & she lost her heart to them. She is an awfully nice girl & knows real people when she sees them. They sent unbounded love to you.

Tea on Sunday was delightful. I got to St. John's Wood safely. Young Dr. & Mrs. Nelson are sweet. They are English but have been a lot in the U.S. Kathleen has visited Camille Irvine for weeks on end at Mercersburg, as well as knowing Kittsie. They have two adorable little girls. Dr. Nelson's mother was there & said, "I hope you may meet in Bulawayo my dear little friend Lorna Tredgold." I said, "I am visiting her!" So it was most amusing. Kathleen's brother was there, Darcy Sullivan, very nice. He escorted me home & asked if he could call, & lo & behold he came yesterday & took Kavie and me out for cocktails & we had a grand time.

Woodie has gone, grâce à dieu.

Yesterday I went to the City to the Union Castle line & got everything fixed up. Kay Mason [a Stonington friend living in London] *went with us & we took Kavie to the Royal Exchange, Bank, Temple, etc. & had lunch at the Cheshire Cheese. She adores London.*

I have a list of cable addresses for you in case you need them for my trip. Dates are the same as I gave you before. Must go now to Kay Mason's for tea. So much love darling & do hope you are happy & enjoying Philadelphia & keeping well. Please share this with Marjorie.

Helen

Poor Woodie! One almost feels sorry for him enduring such a lecture from those young women. Helen certainly wasn't going to waste her time with a man who embarrassed her. In fact, the second part of her letter shows how much she enjoyed connecting with who she called 'real' people, making new friends, and turning almost every gathering into a party. Marvelously, confirming her reservation with the Union Castle Line turned into a City sightseeing excursion and lunch at the Olde Cheshire Cheese pub, still going strong on Fleet Street today. This knack for sociability would be as vital to her trip as all that luggage.

Obviously, we can see from this letter that communications were going to be problematic. We can hardly understand not being able to reach friends and family almost immediately today. But, in 1934 it was a hit or miss situation. Letters to and from London took about a week, but that would change considerably for long shipboard journeys and Africa. Telegrams worked fairly well, and in London the telephone worked very well. It is interesting to imagine all the preliminary arranging Helen must have done to have so many phone numbers in her address book. Hotels and travel companies helped by holding mail and messages. However, the further away from home Helen traveled, the longer it would be between letters. No phone calls, texts, or emails; nor, of course, would she be expecting any. She might have expected a letter or postcard from Al in London, but none had come.

One reason Helen spent almost two weeks in London was to allow time to visit her grandmother, Winifred Odell's mother Martha Kendall. The Kendalls had been living at 39 Castlemaine Avenue in Bournemouth since the turn of the century, but by 1934 the household consisted of only Grandma Kendall and her twelfth child, Beatrice, known as Auntie Trissie, age 47. Winifred's father, Rev. H. B. Kendall, had died in 1919. Helen had visited the Kendalls many times. In fact, when she was four years old, she and her ten year old sister Marjorie spent eight months there while their parents were on a trip around the world, guests of a generous parishioner. And so, on Thursday, January 18, her grandma's ninetieth birthday, Helen caught a train to Bournemouth from London's Waterloo station.

Friday, Jan. 19th
Mother dear,

I am at Grandma's and your two letters just arrived. Was so glad to hear from you. The first few days must have been lonely for you after all the hulla-ballu of Xmas & our leaving, etc. But by now I hope you are more used to it all, and enjoying yourself. You sound very comfy anyway which is something, and you haven't all the packing & unpacking & financial complications that I have in my moving life. It's great fun but very tiring.

After the last letter I wrote to you, Kavie & I went to Kay Mason's to tea (Tues.). The steps are awful, I thought I'd never get up. The apartment drab & very Masony & depressing. Tea was nice. Husband came home & is older looking than I expected – very pleasant but a bit obsequious, trying too hard to be young I think. Kay, I think, is lonely & he may be bored or perhaps just trying to please her because they both are almost a nuisance in asking us there all the time. I've declined all except lunch next Wednesday.

The next day I lunched & spent most of the afternoon with one of the nicest & most attractive men I have ever met – a Dr. John Melly – another friend of Kittsie & Jim's, who looked me up. Then I went to tea at a Mrs. Machado's in Sloane Square, the friend of May Ludlow's, very nice. She had two English girls there, the Misses Arbuthnot – typical very nice English. In the evening I dined & went to see the movie "Thunder Over Mexico" with Betty Odell's [Helen's cousin] *fiancé, Phil Smith & his sister Doris. They are both very nice. I liked them. They have lived a lot in America of course, in fact spent one summer at Groton Long Point & another at Black Point . When I got home about 12 M., I had to pack as the next A.M. I left for here. Kavie left the same morning for Liverpool to visit a friend & we had a very sad parting. She hated to see me go. Her friend in London who was going to do so much for & with her, borrowed 25 pounds from Kavie & sailed for America! So she was a great help, and I too hated to see Kavie go, as she was grand company & I shall miss her and do so hope she'll find some good riding & have some fun over here.*

So I came to Bournemouth, arriving about 2:30. Grandma seems fine, & very little has changed to me in the 3 1/2 yrs. since I've seen her. She's still bright & amusing. She had her best dress & cap on & was surrounded by birthday cards & gifts of all sorts

& enjoying it all thoroughly. She was delighted with your cable. I brought her (en route from station) some beautiful spring flowers & some marvelous grapes, also some books, Sherry's candy, etc. from the ship. Somebody sent her a gorgeous birthday cake with her name & dates on, which we had for tea. Trissie also looks very well & says she feels so now. Several people dropped in to congratulate Grandma. Her birthday has caused a big stir in the community. I was so tired that I had to go to bed at 9:30 & am still there. Trissie brought me my breakfast & so I am remaining here a while as I am still under the weather & should be better by now. The rough trip was the cause I fancy. I shall get up soon. I want to help her & I have clothes to wash & letters – I still haven't got them half done & there are more all the time. Mrs. Bidwell wrote asking me to Feignmouth. Fenza wrote from Paris. Mabel [a Wilmington friend living in England] *has been in a nursing home & goes tomorrow to London, but I shall stop & see Lucy for one night. She sails for Cape Town March 15th. I'll see Mabel in London when I get back.*

I haven't been in a shop since I landed except the florists yesterday & I'm trying to be careful about expenses, but things are dear.

It's very comfortable here at 39 now, with the electric lights & new bathroom, etc. It's very mild out, the sun shining. I have been lucky with the weather. It has rained off & on but not enough to really bother one.

I leave here Monday, spend that night at Southsea with Lucy, get to London Tuesday evening; Wed. will have hair washed, go to bank, etc. & sail Thursday A.M. around 10, at least the train to Tillbury leaves at 10. No one is allowed to go on the train (no visitor) or to see the ship off, so it doesn't make any difference that I haven't many friends or family here. They couldn't come anyway.

Heaven knows when I'll hear from you again but I'll keep on writing as often as I can. You know Alice Murray lives on the Main Line, but I don't know her married name. (I have a feeling that Kittsie knows her, tell Kittsie it's the girl who made shoes, tho she may not remember.)

Well, darling, I hope you can read this. Trissie & Grandma send love & we all wish you were here with us. God & Mary be with you – don't burn the eggs any more. Eat enough. Wear your rubbers

Your ever devoted & adoring daughter Helen.

Helen also decided that before sailing off to Africa she had better write to her sister Marjorie. Her letters to Marjorie were generally more candid and reflect how she was feeling. No need to worry her mother about anything negative, but she could let her hair down to her sister. After all, Marjorie wasn't paying for the trip as their mother probably was. Marjorie was being a good wife and mother to her own three children in Wilmington, not gallivanting around the globe.

Bournemouth
Jan. 19th
Dearest Marje,

Have just finished a long letter to Mother. I feel that she being alone should have the really news letter so you'll have to be content with notes & share hers, otherwise I'd be doing nothing but write, & I'd see nothing.

Having got to London Friday afternoon, I went to Brown Shipley's Sat. A.M. to establish myself as it were, & there much to my surprise was a long letter from you. I was more than delighted but still can't make out how it got here so soon as it didn't come on the Mauretania. *Anyway it was fine & I was thrilled to find it there & I thank you. I certainly would have loved to have seen Anne Dodge & Will out on the same party.*

My London visit was great fun & very busy. Practically all the people I saw were strangers whom I looked up or who looked me up, but it was amusing & they were all nice. The few evenings I didn't step out, Kavie & I dined together & then had a fire in the room & did chores or went to bed & read or talked. For six solid days the world rolled and spun for us after the rough passage over & after a day or so of it, it got our goat so we nearly went batty. It has at last stopped, thank heavens. Also, I haven't slept much. It was so noisy in London, & I got too tired, & got things I had to do on my mind & would ponder them. But here at Grandma's, it is quiet and I am beginning to relax & think I'll get on my feet. The letters bother me so, I haven't thanked even half the people yet who sent me things & now there is Kavie whom I'm afraid is going to be very lonely &

Grandma and Trissie want to hear how & where I am, etc. I wish I had a secretary with me. On the ship I tried to write 4 or 5 letters a day but after the 1st day it got so rough one couldn't write. On the way to Africa we stop about every other day & in between one can see land & will be close so I don't want to miss anything. Oh, well.

London is so gay, such attractive looking people, & twice as many theatres on as we have. They & the restaurants are packed & it seems very gala. I love 'Please' & 'Nymph Errant,' with B. Lillie & Gertrude Lawrence in respectively. There are several other things I am dying to see also an exhibition of British Art, etc. but hadn't time. The weather is warmer than that last winter when we were over, tho it had been cold before I got here.

Grandma is just as cute & bright as ever tho more deaf. But she tells stories & never gets mixed up or forgets names, etc. the way I do. She wants to hear everything about you & the children & remembers everything we've ever told or written her about them. Trissie too looks & is very well. Nobby [Grandma's dog] *has the mange & looks horribly.*

I must stop & get up (I'm in bed.) Please forgive this stupid letter. Someday I'll do better by you. Hope you're all well. Give my love to all the family & my friends you may see.

Much, much love, Marje dear,
Helen

Helen arrived back in London on Tuesday, January 23, after spending the night near Portsmouth with Lucy and her British husband, Douglas Ross. Douglas, an officer in the navy, was about to be stationed in South Africa, and Lucy, plus their two children, would be accompanying him. With only a day and a half left in London, Helen had more errands to do and people to see, as well as packing to do. She couldn't help checking to see if she had any mail at Brown Shipley and discovered at last a letter from Al. Curious that she didn't record what he wrote in her diary, nor did she save the letter. In a final note to her mother she tried to hide her trepidation under the bustle and excitement.

London
Jan. 23rd
Mother dear,

Just a line to say that I am well – had a lovely visit to Bournemouth – one of the nicest I've ever had. It was so pleasant, peaceful and utterly satisfactory. Spent last night with Lucy. It was also awfully pleasant, her children are sweet. Mabel was in London but Sherry came for dinner. I am now in London & Mabel is spending the night with me. Norton Ritchey just stopped in & called. I lunch tomorrow at Kay Mason's, dine with (Dr.) John Melly at his home with his mother & sister! In between I have a shampoo, go to bank, etc. and then leave St. Pancras Station at 10:20 Thursday A.M. & sail around 11 from Tilbury.

I do hope you are well and happy, and enjoying Phila. I sort of hate to embark on Thursday, a step which is taking me further away from you, but it will be a wonderful trip I know, and think when we are together again, what tales to tell. Darling, I do miss you though it's always hard for me to say so or express my feelings.

The best of luck. God bless you and all my love,

Helen

P.S. I went to Burlington House & saw the most wonderful exhibition. Am sending you the catalogue. I looked especially at the Blakes [her mother's favorite artist].

All went according to schedule: the errands, a delightful long lunch with Kay, and an "awfully nice time" but late evening at the Melly's. On departure day, Thursday, January 25th, Helen was up early to finish her packing. Ready to go, she even managed to send a telegram to her mother from the dock. It read:

AM OFF HAPPY LOVE

CHAPTER TWO

On Board the *Llangibby Castle*

H elen's stop-over in congenial England had come to an
end. From this point on she was setting off to regions not
only unknown to her, but virtually unknown to much of
the world. She had planned and packed, booked the best passage
affordable and was ready to employ every bit of her considerable
travel experience. But now, her trip, ostensibly to visit a friend,
was becoming an adventure.

Thomas Cook and Sons had booked Helen on the MV
Llangibby Castle, an intermediate size vessel in the Union Castle
Line's "Round Africa Service." The ship, built in 1929, was 485
feet long, roughly one-half the size of the *Titanic* and, like all of
her sister ships, was named for a British castle, this one in the
southeast corner of Wales. Since 1900, the Union Castle Line
had the Africa route locked up, providing three levels of service,
including the Royal Mail. The East Coast Round Africa Service,
which began in 1910, departed London once a month, traveling through the Mediterranean, down the east coast of Africa,
around the Cape of Good Hope, and back up the west coast,
making stops along the way. These East Coast ships offered First
Class and Tourist accommodations. A First Class ticket to Cape
Town in 1934 on the *Llangibby Castle* is said to have cost £105,
about $525 (or close to $10,500 in 2022). Unless she was going

to fly, like the tobacco businessman Mr. Williams, Helen's only alternative was sailing on a Union Castle ship, especially since Beira on the east coast was her destination. Twenty-nine vessels made up the Union Castle fleet in 1934.

MV **Llangibby Castle,** *a Union Castle Line ship in the "Round Africa Service." (Wikipedia.com)*

The Cunard Line used to tout the slogan "Getting there is half the fun" in order to promote voyages on their ships, and in their case, it was probably true. I'm not sure Helen would have agreed when it came to the *Llangibby Castle.* But then again, I'm not sure Helen knew what half the fun of her whole trip would be. However, she quickly realized that she was in for a new and challenging experience. She may have expected the lush shipboard life of trans-Atlantic travel with nothing to do but meet intriguing people and party night after night, but, as she wrote later, her expectations were shaken on the first day:

"Reality is so often more difficult to grasp than unreality – fact than fiction. It was certainly so for me that early morning of January twenty-fifth. I found myself sitting in a taxicab being driven through the streets of London to St. Pancras Station. Beside the driver I could see my luggage piled up precariously, the fresh red and white tags bobbing in the breeze; the fresh labels already becoming loose at the edges. I could still taste the glue in my mouth from the recent licking and remembered being warned as a child that glue was made from the insides of horses' hooves. I pulled my large fur collar up over my mouth to keep the chill fog out of my throat. My dressing case and golf clubs were beside me and their red and white tags stared at me.

The Llangibby Castle *– sailing from Tilbury January 25th, disembarking - Beira, Portuguese East Africa. It didn't seem possible. I felt as if the tags were on me and wondered why I was going there. Some reason there must have been to have got me this far from the United States, but no very good reason that I could think of. Nevertheless, I was on my way, and in fact, at about that stage of my ruminations, the ancient vehicle I was in suddenly made a gallant last gesture and rushed up the incline to the station entrance in majestic style, attempting to deceitfully demonstrate to the waiting porters her youth and power. I stumbled out and automatically began counting - one, two, three... Yes, right, eight pieces of luggage and one more to be found, I hoped, on the ship. When I sailed from New York, one of my friends surveying my luggage had asked me why I hadn't brought a rowboat too. It might come in useful sometime as well as all the other paraphernalia. Each time I counted my pieces of luggage after that, and it was many scores of times, I remembered the* *remark until I almost felt I did have a rowboat. The porter loaded everything on his van and I followed him into the station.*

Once inside, suddenly it was as if I had opened the cover of a book, one of those many books on Africa, and commenced the first chapter, only I tried to keep impressing upon myself, I was in the book, an actual character in the book. And for the next five months I continued to find myself wandering through this same book as a very minor character but nevertheless there in the setting which to me always seemed more fictitious than real.

So the first chapter opened with the turmoil and excitement of the railway station. Porters dashed here and there; women with children clinging to their skirts tried nobly to attend to them and their rug cases, baskets, valises, tickets, passports; young men carrying shiny new tin cases, no doubt containing spotless new pith helmets, tried to avoid the eyes of their mothers who clung to their arms as if they could never let them go. Older men, with sun-lined faces and very worn tin cases, wiped their red noses and greeted an occasional acquaintance. Women in new clothes anxiously guarded their luggage containing more new clothes that were to last them until their next leave in several years. My porter told me to go to the gate and he'd meet me there. On the way there, I was nearly knocked down several times by figures rushing to get one more magazine, the last morning paper one could get on the same morning instead of six weeks late, the last fresh sweets one could buy that would be fresh.

At the gate, two men seated at a table inspected and stamped my ticket and passport. I passed through and waited by the train for my luggage. My feet were like chunks of ice, my nose too was getting red I knew, and I felt no matter how many coats or furs one wore, it would be impossible to keep out the bitter damp cold. I paced up and down watching the people. The Union Castle Line discourages people coming down to Tilbury to see off the passengers, so practically all the leave-taking occurs at the railway station. There were sisters, brothers, mothers, fathers, sweethearts – on almost every face was written the pain of parting, and often I had to turn away to keep from sharing their pain and to keep from, even by a glance, intruding upon their privacy. I thought of the war and thanked God that at least most of these people would be coming back some day. It was very nearly time for the train to leave and still my luggage had not arrived. I began to get very nervous; I asked several porters what I should do. They said to wait. I asked a Thomas Cook's man to help me find it; he said he was busy. I suddenly felt very much alone and quite unable to cope with the long trip ahead of me with its many probable difficulties. I was cold. The whistle piped. Doors began to shut. What was I to do? Go without it or stay and miss the ship? Everyone else who was going was in the train but me. Damn the porter! And then, all of a sudden he was there – smiling – and quite unruffled. I couldn't speak, but jumped in the train and grabbed the pieces as he tossed them on. The train pulled out. Another fence was over.

There was one seat in the Pullman. Across the little table from me was a pleasant-faced young woman probably about thirty years old, although she looked younger at first glance. She had light fluffy hair which burst out from under her small hat. She too had a fur coat wrapped tightly around her with the collar turned up. 'I say, it is cold, isn't it?' she said. I agreed. We conversed for the hour that it took us to reach Tilbury. She, being English, according to tradition,

should have been the reserved and aloof one, and I, the American,
should have started the conversation and told her my family his-
tory. But it was the reverse. She told me that she wrote for various
English women's magazines, that she was divorced and why; that
she owned a small cottage near Oxford; that she was only going on
the ship as far as Palma; that she was going to find sunshine, copy,
and fun. I told her I was an American and was going to Beira. She
told me she was frightfully bricked to find a friend so early in the
trip. I smiled and muttered something unintelligible.

We arrived at the dock and found porters. I counted eight pieces
without the rowboat. Together we boarded the marine and white
ship, with red funnels, which was waiting patiently for us. I found
my cabin. It was about the size of a modern New York hotel bath-
room only it had a porthole. Out of my eight pieces of luggage, I was
able to keep my dressing case and one small suitcase and a hat box.
The rest went to the luggage room, which was open for an hour each
morning. Even that first day the shifting from winter to summer
clothes loomed large and menacing in anticipation. I met my stew-
ardess, a brusque, starched little dark-eyed pixie. My steward was
an ingratiating worldly man who commiserated with me over the
size of my cabin. 'I saw from your trunk, which has arrived, that
you came over on the Mauretania,*' he said. 'This must seem very*
small indeed after such a ship.' I agreed, but inwardly felt relief
that there was only one berth so that no matter what happened I
could not have a cabin mate forced upon me as I had heard is quite
possible if there is room.

There was no heater of any sort so I felt that I must find some
place in which to thaw out. I ventured forth down the corridor

*and up the main staircase which brought me directly into the main
lounge. But apparently there was no heat here either, and people
were constantly coming in and out from the deck bringing with
them icy blasts of wind. As there seemed to be no other room con-
nected with the lounge, I went on deck and walked aft where I
found the smoking room. It was a small room with no fire and no
obvious means of heating and with three doors opening onto the
deck. This is no better, I thought, and as I can't get external heat,
I'll have to have it internally. I called the steward and ordered a
whiskey and soda. He looked at me dubiously, then raised his eyes
to the wall behind me. He continued to do this without moving to
fill my order, so I turned around to where his eyes rested and read,
'Ladies not permitted in the smoking room.' Rage welled up within
me. I was furious. Was this 1934 or had I made a mistake? 'Is there
another smoking room and bar for ladies?' I asked. 'No, madam,'
he said. 'Very well,' I returned. 'Then I shall remain here unless
I'm bodily ejected.' He looked at me resignedly and moved slowly
away. 'Make it a double whiskey,' I called after him. So I won and
got quite warm both from anger and whiskey. Later in the day, I
returned and brazenly seated myself in the room, the only woman
present. A short time after, a man and woman peeked in, saw me,
so both came in and sat down. Other women followed, and for the
rest of the trip, I and many other women used the smoking room
whenever we wished. I learned that it is a rule of the line to keep the
room for gentlemen only, but some captains are lenient and don't
enforce the rule. Our captain fortunately was amongst this number.*

*The whistles blew, bells rang. 'All ashore' was reiterated. I went
on deck and watched the gangplank hoisted off. Lines were tossed*

off into the water. We were off. A few people stood on the dock waving handkerchiefs. A woman stood near me by the rail quietly weeping. I watched the face of a man on the dock as he waved tragically to another woman, a titian-haired ultra-smart woman near-by. Later I understood his tragedy, for he was forgotten by her within a few hours.

A bugle sounded, and I went to lunch. My friend on the train, Mrs. Tailyour, met me on the stairs and said she had got seats for us both at the same table. So I followed her into the dining room. There were six of us at the table. I was in the middle of one side with Mrs. Tailyour on my right and a young boy on my left. Opposite were an elderly Scotch woman with an unmarried daughter of about 32 or so and a single woman of about fifty. I felt so sorry for myself but more so for the lad on my left. I smiled at him and made some stupid pleasantry concerning the weather I suppose. He looked so petrified that I dared not venture another remark to him the rest of the meal. It was a decidedly painful luncheon, and the food filled me with such misgivings, very well-founded misgivings too, for the future five weeks. Seventy more meals just like this. I pushed the thought away as hard as I could but it persisted. 'No smoking permitted in the Dining Salon,' screamed at me from the menu to add to my despondency. Mrs. Tailyour and I left as soon as we could and had our coffee and cigarette in the lounge, having procured with difficulty two seats. It was easy to see that there were many more people than there were seats and I foresaw a race every day after lunch and dinner – also a foresight well founded.

The afternoon was spent by me in resting in my cabin wrapped up in blankets and coats and in unpacking. My wardrobe was

about two feet high so my evening frocks had to hang from a hook
at the foot of my bed. The skirts of the dresses I pushed through the
two inch space between the footboard and wall. My bed was under
the porthole and was the exact width of the cabin, but it was a short
bed. Next to the foot was the wardrobe, next to the head a small chest
of drawers. When you opened a drawer there was no place to stand
except on the bed. Next to the wardrobe was the door, and in the
corner by the chest was a wash bowl which now and then provided
hot water as well as cold. There was a folding straight chair but
even folded, there was nowhere to put it except on the bed, so I had
it removed. The cabin was always spotlessly clean and light so it
had some good points.

Tea was served at four o'clock in the lounge and the dining
room. There was always a great rush for the lounge on account of
smoking. That first day I had tea alone in the lounge wrapped up
in my big coat. At six-fifteen I had my bath and dressed for dinner.
While [I was] dressing, my stewardess came and said, 'May I have
your bottle, please?' Good God, I thought, how do they know I have
a bottle of scotch? Have they searched the room? Is this another
rule? Each moment of the day I had felt more and more as though I
were back in school. 'What bottle?' I asked as innocently as I could.
'Your bottle for tonight,' she answered. It was a new one on me,
then slowly it dawned. 'Oh, my bottle. Certainly. Just a moment.'
And proudly I dug out a brand new, hitherto unused, mauve hot
water bottle, which a kind friend had presented to me as a parting
gift. A very fortunate thing too, I thought, for as well as being
much needed, I believe that if I had told the stewardess that I didn't
possess a bottle, she would certainly have raised an alarm or else

have dropped dead. When I went up to dinner, all along the passage-way on stands were literally hundreds of hot water bottles, each tagged with the owner's name. I grew accustomed to seeing them after a while but, for the first few nights, I was terribly amused.

Before my stewardess went off with my bottle, I told her about breakfast. I said that I would have it in bed and would ring. 'I'm sorry, Madame,' she said, 'but we are not allowed to serve breakfasts in a room without an order from the doctor saying the passenger is ill.' My heart sank. Seventy meals at that table in the dining room had I said? Good Lord, it would be 105. I couldn't do it. I couldn't. 'What time do you wish your early tea?' she asked. I never had taken early tea, but I had an idea. 'Couldn't you bring me my tea a little late and just slip an orange, maybe, and a piece of toast and some marmalade on the tray with it?' I asked in a hushed voice as though I were a convict trying to urge my guard into a breach of discipline. Well, she thought she might though with great reluctance. It worked well. By the end of the week, I was even getting a half grapefruit or orange juice and several pieces of toast.

I met Mrs. Tailyour in the smoking room for a cocktail, and she asked me to call her by her Christian name and asked me mine. Hers was April, which made me feel just a little bit ashamed of my common Helen. Dinner was as bad as lunch. After dinner was even worse, so I retired very early to my bed and bottle. And so ended my first day."

It's little wonder that Helen sounded dissatisfied with conditions on the *Llangibby Castle*, a striking comparison to the embarkation on the *Mauretania*. No crowded *bon voyage* party, no lavish gifts, no exquisitely polite waiter. She did report to her sister Marje that she had received three cablegrams and "a nice long letter" from Al, but those were all she had to ward off feelings of loneliness and regret. Her closet-like cabin was probably less than half the size of a Cunard First Class cabin and wouldn't have held many champagne-swilling friends in any case. Helen's expectations were based on her previous eight trans-Atlantic round-trip crossings on "luxury liners," as they were referred to. First Class passengers on that route invariably included young Americans, adventurous debutantes, and some eligible bachelors, who were primed for five days of non-stop fun. Actually, this shipboard fun was beautifully spoofed in the Cole Porter/ P.G. Wodehouse musical *Anything Goes*, which opened on Broadway in the fall of 1934. Alas, the prospects on the *Llangibby Castle* had Helen down. However, her diary entry on day three, Jan. 27, showed some hope, "Pretty boring, but early yet." Nevertheless, she began a letter to her mother, pouring out her frustrations and misgivings as the ship headed west through the English Channel toward the Atlantic:

Jan. 26th
M V Llangibby Castle
Dearest Mother,

I must start a letter to you and tell you my impressions as they occur to me, tho it will be a long time before I can even post it. I wrote Marje & several other people to send off by the pilot. They had a sign up that letters should be ready at 5:30. I took mine down at 5, & it was too late. I was furious.

This ship is run like a military camp or girls' boarding school. If you are not at breakfast at 8:30, you don't get any. Fortunately they don't call tea & toast breakfast so my stewardess brought me that this A.M. reluctantly, then told me I'd better get up before cabin inspection. Lunch is at one, dinner at seven promptly. You don't get any if you are late. The food is terrible, bad English. It was so cold yesterday & there is no heat aboard. Every steward & stewardess & passenger last night was running around filling hot water bottles. It was a scream. I'd bet $100 there wasn't one bed without its bottle. Even I, not to be outdone, got mine out. Another rule is – all lights out on the ship (public rooms) at 10:30, unless there's a dance! I guess I'll get plenty of rest. The deck chairs are like our garden deck chairs only no foot rest which I miss. I like to have the legs up, & no rugs [blankets]. All the people brought their own & cushions, etc. & altho' it is cold today, many are on deck, all wrapped up & doing embroidery or crocheting. I wish you could see some of the costumes! I don't consider it rough at all after the Atlantic, but half the people are ill & think it's awfully rough. The service is awful. You can ring all day for someone in the cabin or lounge & no one thinks of coming. You have to go & find them & fairly hit them over the head to get anything, and they are quite impertinent & almost insolent. I am awfully surprised. They are doing us a great favour to take us apparently. No women are allowed in the smoking room without a man. No children allowed above B deck. Isn't it odd? I really don't mind any of it as it's all so different that I am quite intrigued, but I'll no doubt be sick of the ship after a whole month.

My friend is (Mrs.) April Tailyour, believe it or not & it's her real name. She's young & divorced & writes, is very nice. Also have met one man, a sardonic & very rude retired army officer, only going to Gibraltar. April gets off at Palma. We haven't even been gone 24 hours, so that's all I know so far. My table is awful save for April – on my left is an unattractive shy youth who looks so frightened when I speak to him that I don't speak any more. April is on my right & across three very mediocre elderly women, some of them get off along the way so maybe I'll do better later on.

Jan. 30th

It's a beastly cold windy day, and I have a cold, the first in about 6 years. More in my throat than head & really not very bad but annoying. I think it's more the dust in Tangier than anything. It was so interesting though yesterday. I loved it. We got to Tangier at nine & went ashore. I was with April & Captain Cogan (the aforementioned army man). We just wandered about & I was fascinated by the Moors & veiled women, donkeys, beggars, etc. All just as I had imagined a Moroccan town to be. It was quite warm & sunny too. I took some pictures which I hope will come out. We had lunch on the ship & steamed across to Gibraltar, getting there at 3. Again I was thrilled & impressed & not at all disappointed. We walked all over the place. I said last night that I felt as if I have walked all over Europe and Africa in one day – Ces Anglais! We were in Gib. until six. Had tea, etc. & then back to the ship. I was so delighted to find a letter from you in my cabin, also one from each member of the Wellburn family which I enjoyed thoroughly. Do thank them for me.

The crowd on board seems even worse than I thought instead of better. They are so common & rude on the whole. I have talked to various older women & men. The only passable looking ones are the devil to get to know. Capt. Cogan got off at Gibraltar. There is a boy from Halifax who is lame & rather morose but nice & I like talking to him. His name is Dwyer. He & I & an old gent named Dr. Densham & a terrible woman have played bridge but the woman is so beyond words that we have given up that combination. April & fifty other people get off tomorrow at Majorca, but more than 50 get on at Marseilles the next day. I am told that the 'best' English people go by train to Marseilles to embark as it saves them 2 or 3 days of the ship, so I hope things will pick up after that.

Don't think because of my complaints that I'm not enjoying it. I'm having a marvelous time & enjoying it all thoroughly. I told you I'd tell you about my clothes. Since I left N.Y., I have taken turns wearing – brown suit, red suit, black & white suit, blue tweed skirt with blazer. I have worn the red suit an awful lot & am glad I brought it. It will be another week or so before I even open the trunk of summer clothes. In the evenings I wear my three black dresses, my green velvet & the coral dress with jacket from Best's [on Fifth Avenue in New York].

There really isn't much to relate. Tea is about to be served & the women are putting away their embroidery and crocheting. Everyone is rushing for a chair (there aren't as many chairs as there are passengers) & they all eye each other with animosity. I'll have to have mine here on the deck.

And so, my dear, I am thinking of you probably just getting up about now, and am hoping you are keeping well and enjoying yourself.

I send you so much love and then some more love and then
even some more,
Helene

Helen didn't go into much detail about her morning in Tangier, but in a later journal, she described the ship's arrival that day:

"Our first port of call was Tangier. The sun was shining on our first sight of the blue Mediterranean. The white buildings glistened, and the minarets sparkled in the clarity of the day. It was my first sight of an Eastern city, or at least one with an Eastern aspect. Oddly though, it looked to me like a white-washed New York or Miami perhaps. The buildings were tall and built on the sides and tops of the hills and gave the effect of being taller than they are. Those on the top, seen from a distance, assumed the height of skyscrapers. To me, it was very strange. But I soon was distracted by the arrival of the tenders filled with Arabs chattering and grunting and gesticulating, who boarded the ship in droves, their robes flying in the breeze."

Helen's fellow passengers, April Tailyour and
Captain Cogan, on the terrace of the Hotel Villa
de France in Tangier, January 29, 1934.

She also mentions in her diary that she, along with April
Tailyour and Captain Cogan, stopped for coffee at Tangier's Hotel
Villa de France, an elegant old hotel with a garden on the Rue
de la Liberté. It's possible that either April or the captain knew
that Eugene Delacroix had stayed there in 1832 and that Henri

Matisse spent months there in 1912. His painting, *Window at Tangier*, recreates the view of white buildings against that brilliant Mediterranean blue seen from his room. The Villa de France has recently been restored after being abandoned for years.

From the letter to her mother, it was clear that Helen was taken aback by what she called the other passengers' rudeness. But traveling on a Union Castle ship was not a carefree vacation for most of them. She must have been expecting an atmosphere of sociability. In fact, it was more like business as usual. Most of the passengers were either heading to new posts in Africa or returning from leave in England. They knew what to expect from the Union Castle Line and so brought along their own items to make the journey more comfortable. Like commuters on a train, they were far more interested in settling themselves for the requisite trip than making pleasantries with a young American woman, Helen being practically the only non-Brit on the ship. As she was told, a new, perhaps more sophisticated, group would be boarding at Marseilles. This would include notables such as: Sir Harold MacMichael, K.C.M.G., D.S.O., the newly appointed Governor of Tanganyika, and Lady MacMichael along with her maid; Lord Maclay, a shipping magnate from Glasgow; and Baron Cederstrom and his wife, the Honorable Hermione Fellowes, a cousin of Winston Churchill's. That evening, after mailing her letter and playing a little more bridge, Helen noted that she "met the group of stags and danced to Day & Night!" She must have been so excited that she mixed up the name of Cole Porter's famous song. "Night and Day" was one of the hits in the Broadway musical, *Gay Divorce*, starring

Fred Astaire, which had opened in the end of 1932. Although she didn't comment on it, at least we know the *Llangibby Castle* must have had a small orchestra.

A large part of shipboard travel consists of studying the other passengers and becoming wrapped up in their activities, even making up scenarios about them, and Helen admitted to doing this, probably out of boredom.

"And so the next day, and the following days, I spent my time chiefly in observing my fellow passengers. I became interested immediately in watching the titian-haired woman who had been near me on deck when we sailed. She tied up the first day with a retired Air Force commander, who looked more like a successful broker – a large, rather handsome man who showed the effect of high living in his florid rather coarse face. Under the nose of his sophisticated, attractive wife, these two carried on a whirlwind affair in an obvious, oblivious way. From their appearance, I would have expected that experience would have polished up their technique and that they would have used some subtlety, but not at all. The wife was forced to rely on a diabolical looking elderly man, whom she had apparently known before, to keep her from having to appear the humiliated wife, left all alone.

The 'vampire' was perfect for her type. She was tall, thin as a rail, with hands carefully tended, long thin fingers with nails of such a dark red that they appeared almost black. Her face was ashen white, heavily coated, I imagine, with a liquid white powder, her hair the very dark red – or more a dark brown – with a henna or russet tint to it. Her lips were the dark red of her nails. One evening she wore a tight-fitting cloth of gold long dress with a high neck, train, and long sleeves. Around her shoulders was a mink wrap. Another evening, she wore cream-colored satin. The effect would have been superb in a beautiful candle-lit room, or on the stage. On the Llangibby Castle, *with its un-shaded lights, its crowds of plain people, its blasts of cold air, the picture glaringly lacked its setting. She was going to Kenya. The commander and wife were getting off at Palma. We wondered what would happen after that to her on the ship, if she would find another victim. We wasted our time. On the morning of our arrival at Palma, there was a great commotion on B deck. She had decided to leave the ship and stay in Palma too. Stewards were rushing to the luggage room, trunks and bags were brought up. She left us. What happened afterwards perhaps I shall never know. Did the wife just placidly accept it? Did somebody poison somebody? I don't know."*

In any event, Helen slowly began making acquaintances, meeting people and chatting on deck, having cocktails before dinner and even playing roulette at night. She met a couple, Dr. and Mrs. Latham, traveling to Tanganyika Territory with their children, Michael and John, who weren't allowed above B deck. She also got to know another family, the Hillier-Holts, who, along with their three daughters and a nanny, were on their way to Cape Town. And one evening she had drinks with a group that included Jean Campbell, the niece of Sir Harold McMichael, the new governor of Tanganyika Territory. Things were definitely looking up. Marseilles had also brought her "a sweet cable from Al" as well as the more interesting passengers, a fact that she neglected to mention in her next letter.

Feb. 5th

Dearest Mother,

I forgot just when I wrote you last but I believe just before Marseilles. We weren't there very long, but a Miss Ewart & I went to Basso's to lunch. It was very cold out, but the place is mostly all glass, so that the sun through it was really warm and seemed to even get through our clothes a bit. Also the lunch had some real taste to it after this tasteless food, so we enjoyed it. The next day we got to Genoa and it was the coldest day we have had yet. I had such a terrible cold that I only went off for a short walk in the afternoon. In the evening I went with two men [Dwyer and Lieutenant McDermott] *to a cabaret which was quite amusing. The ship didn't leave until the next morning. I wore two sweaters under my coat & froze. Nobody enjoyed Genoa on account of the weather, which is a pity as it's a very interesting place. Fortunately I've been there before. The next day I had to stay in bed my cold was so bad. The stewardess runs all over after me even now giving me some horrible brown mixture & she rubs my chest & puts plasters on me, but I can't see that I'm any better. Warm weather & sun are the only things which will cure me I guess.*

There is an American woman on board who lives half the year in England, a Mrs. MacMillan. She is very nice & happens to have the cabin next to me.

Feb. 6th

What a change the sun makes! I am out on deck & really warm and already my cold seems better. I can almost feel it leaving me. Everybody is bright & cheerful & it seems like a different world.

Last night I sat with a Mr. & Mrs. Hutton & some other people & danced. The former are very nice. They disembark at Beira & go on the same train I do to Bulawayo, only they go beyond.

There is an American on board named Mr. Frazier Jelke. He was in Nassau last winter, since then had a very sensational divorce. He has married children. He has also dyed his hair since last year. He is with a young blonde American – all the ship is much amused. He keeps looking at me (We met several times in Nassau.), but we haven't spoken on this trip. I guess he never expected to see someone he knew on the Llangibby Castle.

We are just passing Crete & after each 3 words I leap up to look at it. It's too beautiful. The mountain tops are covered with snow, and the whole thing has a thing that looks like a rainbow behind it. The sun on the mist from the snow I suppose. The other night I got up & looked at Stromboli [a volcanic Aeolian island] *as we passed, but it wasn't working so there was no red glow. I also saw Sicily as we went through the Straits of Messina.*

We get to Egypt to-morrow. It is lunchtime so must stop. You may think of me now, over my cold, warm & happy. I sincerely hope this will find you the same, dear Madame.

All my love, sweetheart. Hope I'll have a letter from you soon again,

Helen

Mr. and Mrs. Hutton on the deck of the **Llangibby Castle.**

Actually, Helen's cold was not better. And on February 7th, when the ship landed in Port Said at the entrance to the Suez Canal, she went with some of her new friends to the large Simon Artz department store on the waterfront and purchased cough medicine and Kleenex. She also bought a pack of twenty-four small photos of the area. She wanted to be ready for her first land excursion the next day across the desert to Cairo and Giza.

Feb. 12th

Mother dear,

    Today is so hot that people are in tennis dresses & no stockings & all the men in shorts with their topis [pith helmets] *so I feel that I am at last in the tropics. The water looks like oil. Tomorrow morning we arrive at Aden. The swimming bath is up but it is so tiny that it doesn't tempt me very much.*

    To go back to my Cairo trip, I went ashore at Port Said for a little while, went to bed at 11:30 & was called at 2 A.M. There were 14 of us who went. In my car was a boy named Scott – simply sweet who looks like George Darrell [a Stonington friend]. *He is traveling with his uncle Lord Maclay. He is about 25 I should think. Then there was an old lady named Miss Gibbs who came straight out of Cranford* [refers to the 1851 Elizabeth Gaskell novel]. *No words of mine could describe her, and the 4th in our car was an old gentleman named Mr. Hill. If you can imagine an odder four setting out in the dark with a driver who didn't speak English. It was a Buick & very comfortable but cold. Mon dieu, I had two sweaters on, my brown jacket & my brown top coat, a big fur rug which was lent me. What a ride! From 3 to 8:15, but when dawn broke it was unspeakably beautiful and the silhouettes of the figures on camels, etc., the palm trees & huts as it got lighter were something I'll never forget. We had breakfast at Shepheard's* [hotel in Cairo], *and at nine set out to see the pyramids. I got a camel of course; his name was Yankee Doodle, of course. You have seen the Pyramids & Sphinx so you know about that. Then we went to the museum & saw all the Tutankhamen collection. It is too marvelous. I could have stayed there for hours, but unfortunately there was little time. Then we went to the Citadel & the Mosque, & to the Bazaars & back to Shepheard's for lunch at 2. At 3 we left for Suez, 4 hours across desert & such a bumpy, dusty road! When we got there they said the ship was held up in the canal & wouldn't be there till nine, so we had to go to a horrible hotel & we all played rummy & had dinner. It was funny! Everybody was utterly dead, but Scottie, old Miss Gibbs and me. I stayed up until 12 having a drink & relating my experiences to my group of friends. Some people advised me not to go, thinking it too short a time & too expensive & tiring, etc., but I wouldn't have missed it for anything. I wasn't tired & it was a seven pounds well spent I think.*

I read in our wireless news that it is 16 below zero in New York. What a winter. Well, believe me I've had my fill of cold & am so darn glad to be hot I don't know what to do.

There is now a small crowd that I am with most of the time. Mr. & Mrs. Hutton, Mr. & Mrs. Jardine & a Mr. Doxat. The three latter are young, about my age at least, the men in the service & going to Uganda after their leave. The Huttons are older & are just on a pleasure trip. Of course I know everyone else & often join up with other people too. It's all so much more fun now that it's warm – it's like a different ship. People have opened up and are so much more sociable. There are deck sports & dancing & on Wed. is the inevitable fancy dress ball.

I haven't heard from anyone since Marseilles so hope you are all alright. I'll be so glad to have some news again. I hope you get my letters fairly regularly but imagine that they don't get back from these ports very quickly.

All my love darling,
Helen

Pyramids sightseeing party on February 8. Helen is fourth from left on camel "Yankee Doodle."

What a whirlwind trip! Egypt in a day. The customary tourist photo in Helen's album shows the group posed in front of the Sphinx and one of the pyramids, most people on camels, one on a mule, and an elderly couple in a cart. The men seem to have been given fezzes

61

by the smiling camel drivers. Helen, bundled up in her fur-collared coat, looks happy and relaxed on Yankee Doodle next to Miss Gibbs wearing a tall Cranford-type bonnet. Helen took her own snapshots of the Sphinx and camels on the horizon. Unfortunately, she did not take any photos of the glamorous Shepheard's Hotel. This would have been the original Shepheard's that was built in 1841 and then was destroyed by fire during anti-British riots in 1952. Throughout its history, Shepheard's was a gathering point for British colonials, army headquarters during various wartimes, and a magnet for traveling intellectuals and aristocracy alike. Breakfast and a late lunch at Shepheard's, followed, no doubt, by a look around the famous terrace for a familiar face or perhaps a celebrity. Helen's parents had stayed at Shepheard's in 1906 during their trip around the world. Joseph Odell wrote in his diary of their arrival at the hotel on New Year's Day night, "a dance in progress – Anglo-Egyptians and American and English officers in evening dress uniforms made a very pretty sight." And, yes, they also had seen the pyramids and had tea on the terrace the following day.

Having passed through the Suez Canal and picked up the fourteen touring passengers, the *Llangibby Castle* proceeded south through the Red Sea. Helen was able to bring out her summer clothes and store her heavy things in her trunk. She even "took a sun bath in shorts with Mrs. Hillier-Holt." For amusement in the evenings, there were "dog races" and dancing. It had only been twelve days since she had heard from her family. However, the letter she had just written on February 12 would take three and a half weeks to reach her mother, who had left Philadelphia to stay in Wilmington. Communication was becoming more difficult.

Nevertheless, Helen had become completely engrossed in shipboard life, giving herself over to chatting, playing deck sports, napping in the afternoon, having cocktails in the evening.

The ship arrived in Aden, Yemen, on the 13th, four days after leaving Suez, and Helen went ashore to a beach with the Hillier-Holts. The next two days, as the *Llangibby Castle* progressed around the Horn of Africa and down the coast of Somaliland – no pirates in sight, Helen played deck tennis in the afternoon and had drinks with Frazier Jelke and his companion, Nina Pearson. Apparently, all self-consciousness had abandoned Mr. Jelke, and he was happy to socialize with Miss Odell.

Feb. 17th
Mother dear,

Now I am on the other side of the equator. We crossed at 10 P.M. last night. Tomorrow we arrive at Mombasa where we remain for three days. I considered going up to Nairobi for the time but it isn't worth it I believe. You leave (by train) at 3 P.M. & don't arrive until 10 the next morning & just have the rest of that day there & come back. Needless to say it would be very expensive and very hot.

I enjoyed my morning at Aden. I went on a drive around with some people & then we went in swimming at a very nice beach. The water was clear & lovely like the Nassau water.

The last few days have been very gay aboard. All the finals of the sports being played off, etc. On Wed. was the Fancy dress ball. I wore that dotted Swiss evening frock (white with black dots). I pulled the jacket in tight, fixed some lace on those metal back hair curlers &

made a high collar, fixed my hair over a pair of stockings to make a pompadour, pinned a bunch of daisies on my little white hat & wore long black gloves. It made a very effective 1900 costume & I was much complimented on it & cheered. I went to a big cocktail party before dinner, then dined with friends & had champagne, etc. It was all very gala & lots of fun. Yesterday the children had their fancy dress party & were too sweet. I assisted & played games with them. In the evening we had a Derby. I was Mr. Dwyer's horse, called Miss North America. I can't explain now how it was done but it was very good sport. I shall remember it for Stonington.

I have thirteen more days on the ship – no eleven it is, and it seems very little. I can't seem to remember or look forward to any other life than this. I'm sure I have always been here. It is funny how one can settle down to it. At least half the people get off to-morrow at Mombasa, & after that the crowd will be changing all the time they say. All the people for Nairobi, Tanganyika, & Kenya get off at Mombasa. I should love to go to Kenya but I can't arrange it very well, the distances are so great. The new governor (& his wife & niece) of Tanganyika are on board – Sir Harold and Lady MacMichael. The niece came down yesterday with measles, so we arrive in port flying the yellow flag. There is much discussion as to whether we will be quarantined but I think now we definitely won't be. I spent almost the entire afternoon with the girl that day & she was covered with the rash then but thought it was prickly heat. In the evening she danced. She is about 20 & very attractive.

Also on board are the Baron & Baroness Cederstrom. The Baron's first wife was [opera singer Adelina] *Patti.*

It is terribly hot today. I have on one of Dassie's tennis frocks with very little underneath it.

There are of course the usual intrigues, jokes, etc., etc., but I can't explain them all in a letter but will try to remember everything to relate to you on my return.

In the meantime I am sorry that much of this trip I can't share with you, some of it I'm glad you were spared such as the cold, & now I think you'd find the heat trying. The ship is only 5 years old but it is old fashioned & was never built for comfort. The shore trips are difficult with many steps and having to stand a great deal of waiting for boats, etc. I am loving it all now, but I think one needs to be young & healthy.

I hope you are retaining your effervescent youth & are healthy. I certainly will be glad to hear from you. Give my love to everybody & no end of it to you darling,

Helen

Had Winifred Odell originally thought about accompanying Helen on this journey? What a different trip it would have been. Helen's mother was sixty-two years old, and I believe that she had already experienced knee and hip problems. She also had a reputation for being slightly difficult, whatever that meant, perhaps moody and a bit sorry for herself at times. Helen obviously was trying to make her mother feel better about not coming along, but then flattering her too. "Effervescent youth" seems slightly odd after pointing out all the hazards of travel she would have to deal with at an advanced age. And it is hard to imagine in the grandmother I knew some twenty years later, but maybe.

The social life on the ship was becoming increasingly busy as well as slightly bawdy. Helen didn't let her mother know that the gala costume evening ended with dancing and singing in the café. "Great fun!" she wrote in her diary, which had a *Llangibby Castle* menu card for the Fancy Dress Ball buffet tucked into the February 14 page. Some wag had written in pencil on the back of the card: "There was a young girl from Pitlockry, Whose morals were simply a mockery, For under her bed, she'd a lover instead, Of the usual piece of white crockery." Limericks and all sorts of clever verse always delighted Helen, and I can almost hear the table's hilarity over this one, while sampling the macaroons and petits fours and sipping champagne. The customary shipboard horse races inspired more silliness. As Helen wrote in her letter, she was Mr. Dwyer's "horse" in the Derby. However, she omitted some of the horses' full pedigrees: 'Miss North America, by Skiing out of Snow,' 'Eno's by Stomach out of Order,' 'Evicted by Husband out of Cabin,' for a few.

On February 15th, Helen hosted her own cocktail party, probably in the lounge. Later that evening she played in a bridge tournament and noted, "Lady MacMichael and Baroness Cederstrom so mean to Mr. Carter." Nothing like being ganged up against by two titled British ladies at the card table. As Helen had mentioned to her mother, Baron Cederstrom had been the third husband of the famous opera diva, Adelina Patti. A generation younger than Patti, Rolf Cederstrom, a former lieutenant in the Swedish Light Guards, was directing a health and fitness club in London before marrying and moving to the diva's estate in Wales. After

Adelina's death in 1919, the Baron met and married Hermione Frances Caroline Fellowes, daughter of the 2nd Baron de Ramsey and Lady Rosamond Spencer-Churchill. The Cederstroms were scheduled to disembark the *Llangibby Castle* at Mombasa, most likely in order to visit friends among the crowd of British ex-pats in Nairobi, Kenya.

Helen had talked herself out of the side trip from Mombasa to Nairobi: too much train, not enough time there, and too expensive. This must have been a tantalizing decision, because Helen would have read all about Kenya's racy colonial settlers, otherwise known as the Happy Valley set, in New York and London newspapers. The Prince of Wales and his brother, the Duke of Gloucester, both keen on safari hunting and early airplane flights, had been visiting Kenya. If all these fascinating people were living it up in Nairobi at places like the notorious Muthaiga Club, Helen would have wanted to spend at the very least a day there. But, on February 18th, after saying good-bye to friends getting off in Mombasa, she wrote in her diary, "Ship horrible & deserted. Sort of wish I had gone to Nairobi."

Mombasa, a busy port on the Indian Ocean initially colonized by the Portuguese in the sixteenth century, was inhabited by a diverse mixture of Africans, Arabs, and Indians. The British took control in 1887, and when construction of the Kenyan Uganda Railway began in 1896, many more Indian workers were brought in. Mombasa had been the British East Africa capital, but by 1906, the railway was completed, and Nairobi took over that honor.

Making the best of the three days in "very hot" Mombasa, Helen went ashore with friends. The first day she joined a group going to the private Mombasa Club for a swim and tea, then on to see native dances and parades. On Monday, she went sightseeing with the Huttons to the Indian quarter, Tudor City, the old port, and Fort Jesus, built by the Portuguese in the 1590s and used by the British as a prison. The third day, Helen went with the Hillier-Holts to a hotel further up the beach for another swim and a "really quite good tea." She wrote in her diary, "Lovely ride back in the cool of the evening." She also noted that Julius Fleischmann's (think of yeast and margarine) yacht was anchored in the harbor. Indeed, his 225-foot yacht *Camargo* was on a round-the-world cruise at that time.

Black and white photos in Helen's album show Mombasa's sights, but are oddly unpopulated: a few dhows in the harbor, one native perhaps in costume, some shoppers in the distance at what looks like the marketplace, the only car the one that they had hired. Fort Jesus can be glimpsed behind a large tree, no one around. Now, compared to the many videos of Mombasa on the internet, the contrast is more than striking. With the exception of the fort, not one building in today's Mombasa, even in the Old Town, looks old enough to have been there in 1934. The Mombasa Club still exists but has obviously been updated. The streets of Mombasa today are teeming with cars, trucks, motorcycles, as well as people, a very different atmosphere with a population of over a million.

Feb. 19th

Marje dear,

    We got in to Mombasa yesterday A.M. A lovely entrance with many palm trees, etc. We are tied up to the pier & the huge cranes, about six of them have all got great signs on them "Babcock & Wilcox – London & Renfrew"! [Marje's husband Tom Bradford worked for Babcock & Wilcox.] *We are here until day after to-morrow, a bit long to be sleeping in a tiny cabin with no air. My cabin is on the pier side & the noise & heat are quite something. But, I am fascinated by the place. It is really Africa & really tropical. We have to wear topis always & take quinine daily & sleep under mosquito netting. I wish I could describe the place, great trees with huge trunks & queer moss hanging off them, narrow little streets filled with Swahilis half-dressed and many Indians. People who have been to India say that you wouldn't know you weren't there when in their quarter here. There are many groups of thatched huts & monkeys, also parrots. I took some pictures to-day & do hope they will come out. Yesterday I went swimming all afternoon (from 4-6; one doesn't venture out before four) at the Mombasa Club. You have to swim in pools or netted-in places on account of sharks. Yesterday Mr. Hutton caught a 90 lb. shark right off the side of the ship. To-day I went with the Huttons & a Mr. Clark for a long drive getting in & out seeing things.*

    A lot of the people I liked got off here & have gone up-country so I feel a little lost. A few old stand-bys are here though. It's all devilishly expensive. It costs 10 shillings to get from the ship to the town alone. Each port in fact costs several pounds even if one is taken about some of the time & I've been pretty lucky that way.

I haven't heard a word from America since Marseilles whenever that was, but I guess it is impossible to reach me. We are the only ship down this way in a month, & there won't be another for another month.

My hand is sticking so to the paper that I'll stop now & try to find some air. Am I not thankful for those tennis dresses I had Dassie make? But am I not shuddering at my laundry bill!

Hope you are all well & happy. I'd love to see you but I'm afraid it will be some time before that can be arranged.

Loads of love dearie & some for all the family too,

Helen

Communications were becoming troublesome to Helen. She next wrote her mother a quick note before the end of the voyage and explained the situation. "I find that a letter I wrote Marjorie a few days ago couldn't get to America under five weeks, so I'm sending this by air mail as far as England anyway, and that one to her will come weeks after probably. This East coast is very isolated. It is pathetic to see the English so excited over the arrival of this ship, the only one in a month from England." The sub-equatorial heat was also a concern. "I am now taking my quinine, sleeping under mosquito netting, wearing a topi & when I drink I have a gin & tonic. Every day one person or another disappears with a chill and fever so one does have to be careful.... All the men wear shorts & topis all day, then heavy black dinner coats in the evening & simply swelter. The food on board in the typical English (please excuse me) way is exactly the same as in a frigid clime!! Roast beef, pork, steamed puddings, hot soups. Not one thing suitable. It is so silly."

Leaving Mombasa on February 21st, the *Llangibby Castle* quickly worked its way south along the coasts of Tanganyika and Portuguese East Africa (Mozambique) for the next six days. Tanganyika had been a German colony until the British took it over under the League of Nations Mandate in 1922. (The country achieved independence in 1961 as Tanzania.) Anxious to get on with her trip, Helen made brief diary entries covering those last ports and days on the ship.

Wednesday, Feb. 21

Left Mombasa at 12. Many new people aboard. At six o'clock we got to Tanga. Very pretty from the ship. Didn't go ashore as not many boats & the mosquitoes too dangerous. All Tanga came aboard however. Had to go to bed early to get rid of Hinks [another passenger going on to Capetown.]

Thursday, Feb. 22

Got in to Zanzibar about 11. Beautiful dhows sailing around. After lunch went ashore with Huttons. Wonderful narrow streets, beautiful carved doorways. Only a few hundred white people. Sultan rules. Very pretty & clean. Wild buffalo grazing. Went out to clove plantation & to Sultan's palace where he had 99 concubines. Burned in 1890. Ivory carved here. Bought some presents. [Perhaps some of those tiny ivory animals that we still have.]

Friday, Feb. 23

Got in to Dar-es-Salaam early. Mrs. McMillan and I went ashore & took a rickshaw. Hot! Got stamps. Saw Dr. Latham [Dr. Latham, his wife and two young sons had just disembarked from the *Llangibby Castle.*] *& went in & had tea. They live at Mwanza, Tanganyika* [on Lake Victoria]. *He took us on a drive & back to ship. Dar-es-Salaam was a German colony. One can see the large floating dock they put across the narrow entrance to the harbor to keep the English out during the war. Slept all afternoon. Was pursued by Hinks – old lecher. Danced & drank with many people.*

It seems that Helen and the Lathams had become quite good friends on the ship. I came across a hand-written letter from Mrs. Latham tucked into Helen's photo album. While it was a thank-you note for a card Helen had sent the following Christmas, the letter goes on at length giving a firsthand, and somewhat hair-raising, picture of British colonial life. Admittedly, colonialism takes the blame for many of the world's problems and is today politically incorrect, but it would be hard to hold it against a woman like Mrs. Latham. A word of warning, in the 1930s killing wild animals was considered an enjoyable sport.

Mwanza
Tanganyika Territory
13th Jan. 1935
Dear Miss Odell,

It really was very swell of you to remember us all at Xmas. Your card was a very welcome surprise & I am hastening to convey our appreciation.

First about people you know. The Governor & wife [the MacMicheals] *are not too popular – full of grand ideas about spending money on redecorating Govt. House & buying a new Rolls Royce – as Government money goes into this none of us officials are too pleased. The country is not too financially sound & we feel the money might be better spent. They have covered most of the country & we have had them here twice. Personally we've found them very charming & friendly, but many other people say that they have developed swollen heads. The niece spent about 6 months in the country & was a kind of tornado, she went back via S. Africa & was put off at Durban with suspected diphtheria. She went into the isolation hospital, but after they found it was only septic tonsils, she stayed with the James family & had a grand time.* [Wasn't this same girl who was thought to have the measles in Mombasa?]

I hear from the Brittains occasionally. Anne (the attractive daughter) is marrying soon. Her bloke has a Classics-master post at Eton, so they sound O.K.

Young Pedler (do you remember him?), loaned to this Government for 2 years by the Colonial office, was first in Dar & is now at a lovely station 40 miles away, so I asked him to spend New Year with us. He came, but he started by car at 4 p.m. on the Saturday & only arrived at noon next day!! Swollen rivers, floods & bad roads had done their worst. All he & his boy had to eat were a lb. of chocolates & a small jar of pastilles. As you can imagine he got here filthy & ravenous – his first experience of roads in Africa!!!

We like Mwanza very much. It is on Lake Victoria which of course is incredibly large. Soon after we arrived, we bought a small boat & outboard engine & we have tremendous fun cruising round & almost every Sunday we go off to one of the rocky attractive islands for breakfast. John and Michael are thrilled of course. On these expeditions we invariably see & shoot at crocodiles & twice we have chased the devils through thick undergrowth & eventually got them right up about 200 yds. from water. It is great fun. The females lay their eggs in the sand right away from the lake's edge in a nice cozy spot. You come upon them keeping guard. Don would have a shot from the back & then the brute would start tearing along with a noise like thunder, the kids & myself & a boy or two tearing along behind till the killing shot – then gaze at the kill. One day we unearthed 120 eggs & had great fun smashing them against the rocks.

We have been on one shooting trip to a place 80 miles away. It is just on the edge of a game reserve so there are masses of every kind of beast. We even saw a lion. It was fine for the brats as we let them stay up & yarn round the camp fire at night. As they will soon be off to school, I want them to see as much of the wild life while they can. They are both very bloodthirsty (like father) & delight in the day's hunting & killing.

We get lots of tennis, golf of a kind, & there is quite a decent club. We are about 60 Europeans so have lots of dances & dinner parties & bridge, & life sails along merrily. The only snag is teaching the kids. I give up the mornings to that & find it an awful effort. My plan is to take them home in June. Don will get local leave, take us as far as Durban, have a fortnight with us there & then see us off & wend his weary way back for a year before he is due for leave. I want to put the kids at school in Switzerland for a year; but with the exchange against us, maybe the exchequer will not agree. After that they will be settled at a prep school in England & the trouble begins − the family broken in halves − that is the devil of this country.

I have had masses of visitors lately. We are at the end of the railway with a lake steamer service to the next few Tanganyikan places, & Kenya & Uganda, so there are always people passing backwards & forwards waiting for connections. This is a hospitable country & even people you've never seen either drift in or are rescued from the very miserable hotel. Some, one hopes to see again, others…

We have also had some Parliamentarians touring the country & a party of Public schoolboys. On these occasions we are asked to take a couple, house & look after them. The schoolboys, aged about 17-19, made me feel very ancient. One had fell down the hold of the Lake steamer & cracked his skull. Don had him in hospital for about 6 weeks; but he has recovered & has gone. It is a queer country, full of variation.

We get leave in about August 1936, and having settled the kids at school, we hope to be able to do a trip to the States. We've always longed to, so who knows, we may meet again. Should you ever be this way again, Heaven knows what place we will be in, but you will always be welcome, in fact we should be most annoyed if you didn't break your journey & look us up.

c/o Medical Service
Dar-es-Salaam, T. T.
will always find us.

Hope you are not bored with this effusion.
Kind regards & the best of everything for 1935 from us all.

Sincerely yours,
Gwynneth Latham

The Lathams with a 10-ft, python, shot by Donald (second from right), hanging from the trellis. Son Michael is hold-ing the python's tail. (Photos from Gwynneth Latham.)

John and Michael Latham sitting on a dead
14-foot crocodile on the station platform.

The picture of young John and Michael Latham at school in Switzerland homesick for those fun Sundays smashing crocodile eggs at Lake Victoria is rather haunting. As for the free-spending governor, Sir Harold MacMichael went on in 1938 to become the High Commissioner of the British Mandate of Palestine. He held that controversial position until 1944, both he and Lady MacMichael barely escaping assassination on a couple occasions. But, then, that's a whole different story. Now back to Helen's last few days on the *Llangibby Castle*.

Saturday, Feb. 24

Nothing much. Have ADC [aide-de-camp] *to Gov. of Zanzibar & ADC to Gov. of Uganda at table. So Oxford! Wore magenta dress at night. Rain storm & all my clothes & bed were drenched! Bird* [Major G. F. Bird] *came to rescue.*

Sunday, Feb. 25

Spent horrible morning packing – awful! In the eve. had some champagne which was only bright spot of day.

Monday, Feb. 26
Beira

Finished packing & had drinks with Hinks. Got to Beira [Mozambique] *at 4. The end of* Llangibby*!! What a time at pier – heat & the Portuguese. Too awful for words. Finally at about seven got on train. The nuts next to me! Dinner with Huttons & Bird. Hard bed but fascinating outlook. Moonlight & Africa.*

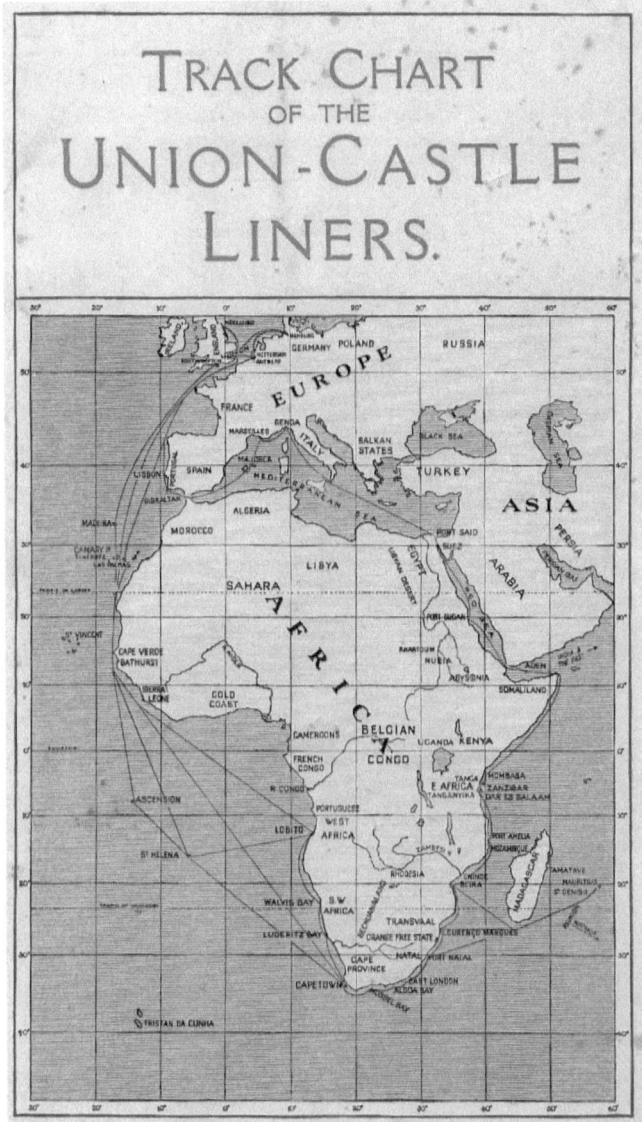

Map showing the routes of the Union Castle liners.
The route through the Mediterranean Sea progressing
down the east side of Africa was the one the **Llangibby**
Castle *followed. (Union Castle Line brochure)*

CHAPTER THREE

Southern Rhodesia

Victoria Fall Hotel,
Victoria Falls,
Southern Rhodesia
March 3rd.
Mother dear,

You will probably be surprised to see where I am but – one never knows.

We landed at Beira a couple of days early for some unknown reason – on the 26th. What a day! It is the hottest, filthiest place full of fever and malaria. The dock and customs place were beyond words, & the old Portuguese too vague but also disagreeable for words. Thank Heavens it was train day, otherwise we would have had to have stayed there for five days. Well, I battled with my luggage, etc. from 4 – 6:30. They soaked me £ 2/- excess weight & about £ 3/- in various taxes, etc. Fortunately I got a compartment in the train to myself. The Huttons, a Major Bird & various other people I knew were also on the train. Bird, Huttons & I had a table together in the diner. It was a good train. I stayed awake most of the night looking out of the window – anyway my bed was so hard my hip bones got black & blue. At six A.M. we reached Umtali on the So. Rhodesia border & the customs man came on & asked many questions, etc. I had breakfast at 6:30. The train stopped quite often but not usually at a station – just a kraal & a few natives would come to the windows to sell peanuts, ears of corn, or tomatoes [according to Helen's diary the train stopped to buy two cabbages for the dining car]. *At 2 o'clock in the afternoon we got to Salisbury, the capital of So. Rhodesia. It looks about like a town in the cowboy moving pictures or perhaps as Fulton* [N.Y. in 1895] *looked when you went there first. At 4:30 we left. The next A.M. at 6:30 (Wed. 28th) we arrived at Bulawayo.*

I, as yet, have had no message from Lorna anywhere. I went to the Post Office & they told me that Box 388 was being emptied every day. I lured them into giving me the Tredgold house & office address (Neither have a telephone.) I went to the office & there was a sign on the door saying Mr. Tredgold was at Cape Town, would return about 25th of Feb. I got a taxi & after much trouble found the house & that it was let to a Mrs. Williams. She said they were leaving the next day as the Tredgolds were arriving back at any moment. She said she got their mail every day. There was one letter for me from the Carnarvon Arms England. I was so disappointed. I have had no word from or of America since January 30th at Marseilles! However, I wrote Lorna & left the letter to say that I was going on to the Falls with friends & to wire me here on her return.

I can't say much for her house – a tiny bungalow, with a tiny garden, in a suburban row of others just like it – a flat outlook chiefly of dust & corrugated iron. I have never seen so much corrugated iron as in this country. I don't think I'll stay there very long, unless of course I have a very good time. As soon as I go back there

I shall try to get passage home as the ships are all packed. Everyone is horrified that I'd come out here without my reservation home! It seems queer to me with the trans-Atlantic ships all empty.

Well, the Huttons & Bird having urged me to come to the Falls with them, I went back to the station, checked my big luggage there & joined them on the train for here at 11 A.M. It was one of the hottest trips I have ever experienced. Out here one travels in cotton dresses, no stockings, etc. The dust & heat ruins anything good on a train. We had lunch & dinner together & arrived here at 10 P.M. and was I glad to get here. It is a lovely hotel. The Huttons say that it is something like the Constant Spring Hotel [in Jamaica] only much nicer. I got a room with a private bath & have never appreciated one more. It's 35 shillings a day inclusive & the meals are excellent. The best food I've had since I left America & how they get it up here I don't know. It's absolutely in the wilderness. The only thing troublesome is that altho my windows & ventilator are screened, one has to sleep under nets & take quinine & can't stay out after six P.M., and it's full moon & quite tantalizing. Also you have to be awfully careful of the sun.

As for the Falls, they are unbelievably beautiful, a mile & a quarter across & 500 ft. drop. The tropical growth around them & the mists & rainbows & all are breath-taking. It is absolutely left in its natural state just as Livingstone found it. There are baboons & monkeys all over the place. There are also lots of hippopotami but I haven't seen one yet. I've seen crocodiles & also a cobra right in the path in front of me! There is a lovely swimming pool & also a nine-hole golf course. I could stay here for a long time quite happily but think I'll probably just stay for about 4 more days if I hear from Lorna before then.

I wish I'd told you to write by air mail. There is air mail from London to Bulawayo & I believe it would be much quicker. I must stop now or this will be too heavy. Please share this with Marjorie. I'm wondering where & how you are. I fancy you'll be leaving Philadelphia soon, but of course I know nothing. You had only been there about a week when I last heard. I wish you were here, you'd love it, but you wouldn't love the getting here.

All my love darling. It will be good to see you again,
Helen

What!? To come all that way and your friends aren't there! Helen must have been in shock. By the sound of her letter, after she had time to calm down, she seemed to be under control and probably didn't want to upset her mother unduly. It all came down to communication. She had the Tredgolds' post office box number but not their actual address, which she had to "lure" the postal clerks into giving out. The tenant, Mrs. Williams, didn't seem to have much information either. It is interesting that Helen apparently did not try to send Lorna a telegram from Mombasa or Beira, and neither did Lorna send a telegram to the ship alerting Helen that they would be in South Africa until after the end of February. All very casual, especially to people today who exchange streams of text messages even as they meet up for coffee. Helen's diary entry for Wednesday the 28th expresses her "horrible disappointment" at finding no Tredgolds, "no mail, no word from Lorna." And her disparaging remarks about Lorna and Robbie's house are surprisingly rude, a peevish first impression, perhaps brought on by the uncertainty created by their absence. Only a few days in Africa and she was ready to go home.

However, Helen was resourceful and quick on her feet. She was not about to hang around a dusty town full of "corrugated iron" waiting for her hosts. No indeed. She made it back to the station, checked her trunk, and clambered onto the 11 A.M. train to join her friends from the ship. At that time, Bulawayo was the largest "city" in Southern Rhodesia, but it certainly didn't look enticing to her. Better to be off to the luxurious Victoria Falls Hotel.

David Livingstone came upon the huge falls as he traveled eastward down the Zambezi River in 1855. The local natives had called the falls 'Mosi-Oa-Tunya,' the smoke that thunders, and it was exactly that smoke or "columns of vapour" that Livingstone first saw signaling the river rushing into a 400-foot chasm. Victoria Falls, named for his queen by Livingstone, is twice the size of Niagara Falls, extending over a mile from end to end. Livingstone wrote in his *Missionary Travels* (1857) that the columns of vapour "were white below, and higher up became dark, so as to simulate smoke very closely. The whole scene was extremely beautiful." Located in the far western tip of Zimbabwe, Victoria Falls has not yet undergone a native name change. However, Hwange, the town and nearby national park just south of the Falls, was changed from the colonial phonetic version, Wankie. The town of Livingstone, formerly the capital of Northern Rhodesia, now Zambia, lies on the other side of the Zambezi River from Victoria Falls.

In 1904 Cecil Rhoades' Cape-to-Cairo railway reached the Falls, and a primitive hotel was constructed overlooking the scenic gorge. By 1915, a more substantial building, encompassing the main lounge and north and south wings, was built. During the 1920s the hotel became a popular tourist destination, and a formal dining room, a swimming pool, and more luxury rooms with private baths were added. In order to make viewing the Falls easier on guests, a trolley running on a two-foot gauge track was installed from the hotel down to a point near the rail bridge linking Southern and Northern Rhodesia. While the trolley coasted downhill, native men pushed it back up to the hotel. By the time I was able to stay at the Victoria Falls Hotel on a trip to Africa in 1994 little seemed to have changed, except that the trolley had disappeared. My photographs look much like my mother's. It was still quite remote but supremely beautiful, luxurious, and very popular. Seen from the wide veran-dah, the view of the Zambezi Bridge, with the mist from the Falls rising beyond it, remains the same.

By the time Helen had written to her mother on March 3rd she had passed three restful days at the Victoria Falls Hotel. Two days on trains plus the fiasco in Bulawayo had left her limp. She and her friends had not arrived at the hotel until 10 P.M. on the 28th – the comment in her diary being, "Thank Heavens a delightful hotel. Drinks & then to bed & to revel in my bath." Her first full day, described in her diary, was spent in the typical way, in fact much like the way I spent mine sixty years later.

*Mrs. Hutton (left) and Helen (right) on the
trolley at the Victoria Falls Hotel.*

*Thursday, March 1 – Up early – good breakfast & off to see
Falls. Too utterly marvelous. Very hot tho. Back on funny little
trolley. In afternoon [we] took boat trip up the Zambezi River to
an island for tea & lots of monkeys there. Back by 6 & in pool.
Cocktails at 7:30. Sat around talking all evening.*

The verandah at the Victoria Falls Hotel.

Two days later things got a little livelier.

Saturday, March 3 – Went to Livingstone with Huttons &
Mr. Spencer, to hospital & Dr. Kirby. Queer town, the capital of
Northern Rhodesia, but it is being changed to Lusaka. On return
we went to Palm Garden but I saw a cobra & fled in terror. Siesta
after lunch. Tea & talked to Mr. Marthoz from the Belgian Congo.
In evening he joined us & I had a H— of a time with him.

Now this story about the snake was told and retold over the
years. It was perhaps Helen's favorite thrilling Africa tale, because
it always got a huge reaction. Palm Grove (not Garden) is on the
Zambian side just down river from the roiling water of what is
called the Boiling Pot. Today it is a white-water rafting launch
area but was probably naturally wild in 1934. As she used to tell
the story, she was walking with friends single file on a path when

the man behind her saw the snake hanging from a tree and pushed her out of the way. Instead of a cobra, it had become a black mamba, very venomous and quick. Her life was saved! Cobra or black mamba, in the path or on a tree limb, time has a way of changing the details, but does it really matter? Drama usually comes with the retelling of stories and absorbing the response – more response, more drama. One story that did not get retold was what a hell of a time she had ditching Mr. Marthoz from the Belgian Congo.

The days at the hotel went on until

Tuesday, March 6 – Mr. Soper took us up the river in his car, then we walked thru long grass to see his croc-trap. On Saturday there was a python on it! Got back & found a telegram from Lorna so spent afternoon packing & paying bill, etc. Tried to photo natives cutting grass & one chased me. They were convicts! Left on six o'clock train, dinner with Huttons. We stopped at Wankie, big mining town. Hard bed & many insects.

32 Borrow St.
Bulawayo
March 7th
Dearest Mother,

Now I am at Lorna's, all unpacked, and settled in. I arrived at 6:30 this morning from Victoria Falls. I was at the Falls for a week, then yesterday got a telegram from Lorna to say they were back so I came with the Huttons on the train, the Tuesday train.

The next train would have been on Friday. I enjoyed the week there immensely. It is awfully quiet, nothing much to do, but the scenery is gorgeous and the hotel good. We walked most of the time, ate & slept.

Lorna & Robbie met me at the station this A.M. I said good-by to the Huttons there after having been with them more or less since Jan. 25th. Lorna seems a little older of course, & has that rather sallow look they all get out here. Otherwise she is just the same. It is ten years since I have seen her! Robbie is not very handsome but I believe I will like him very much. The bungalow is much more attractive than I first thought, small of course, but cool. I have a lovely big room, very attractively tinted in pale blue with a pretty chintz, sprays of flowers on a pale yellow background. There is a tiny wardrobe but not one drawer. I have to keep everything in my trunks & suitcases. There is a bathroom with tub & basin & hot water, but the toilet is about 25 yds. from the house outside. Lorna said that one night as she was going out there, a snake wound itself around her leg but Robbie shot it with a revolver before it bit & killed her! I shall not enjoy going there. Also one has to sleep under nets here too & I don't like that as one doesn't get much air. However, this is Africa. They have three boys – cook & two house boys; 2 cars – a Ford & baby Austin. The garden is small but filled with flowers. It is a funny town, flat as a pancake, all sprawled out & very crude. One sees span of oxen everywhere, also donkeys. I must admit that Africa as I have seen it so far is much less civilized & developed than I expected. Bulawayo is 40 years old. I can't tell you much about the life here yet. I know they always have tea at about 6 A.M., breakfast at about 7:30 I believe. Then always mid-morning tea, lunch at one, tea again at 4:15, Sun-downers (drinks) at about 6, dinner at seven & bed early. I haven't been up much after 11:30 or often 10:30 since I left England, but I have never been up so early in my life.

I had one letter awaiting me from you. It missed me at Marseilles & was sent on here. It was written Jan 22nd, also ones from Al, Harry & Frank Dodge all written about a week later. You had just got back from a week-end at Mrs. Scotts'.

I am in my room taking my siesta having been asleep for about an hour. Always on the ship & here one stays in one's room quietly from 2-4. Now I shall take a bath & get clean after that hot & filthy sleeper last night, & the exertion of unpacking, etc. this A.M. It would be nice to know where you are & what you are doing at this moment. I think I'll send this & all my letters from now on to Stonington. I can't write too long letters at a time or they will be too heavy for the air mail, but I'll be writing again in a few days.

No end of love my darling from your Africana daughter.

P.S. Just lost a colossal filling out of my back tooth. I thought the tooth had dropped out. Lorna says the best dentist in S.A. is here so I'll get it fixed right away.

The Tredgolds' house at 38 Borrow St. in Bulawayo.

Lorna Tredgold in front of a kraal.

The Tredgolds' "house boys."

Almost at once Helen's expectations collided with the reality of her hosts and her surroundings. Her summer friend from ten years earlier was a married woman now, bending to her husband's life and work in an African colony. And that husband didn't quite live up to Helen's mental image of a dashing adventurer from the veldt, based on what? Movies, novels, handsome English princes? Remember, she had never met Robbie Tredgold before. A later description of him in the *Oxford Dictionary of National Biography* records that he was "a man of lean and ascetic appearance and upright carriage. From his sunburnt face piercing blue eyes, under a broad forehead, looked out with an apparent seriousness that disappeared with a shy but ready smile." At least the cottage, with its sweetly decorated guest room and three houseboys, went up in her estimation. But Bulawayo still seemed "less civilized" than her idea of African cities based most likely on stories of sophisticated goings-on in Nairobi and Cape Town.

The Matabele (referred to nowadays as the Ndebele) tribe, led by their chief Lobengula, first settled Bulawayo in 1840, and the name means 'the place of the man who was killed' in Zulu. After two wars with the Matabele, the British South Africa Company incorporated the town in 1897, which accounts for Helen stating that it was only forty years old. She recorded in her notebook that the European, i.e. white, population of Bulawayo was 10,597. However, Europeans represented less than 5 percent of the total population of Southern Rhodesia at that time. In a book about his life published in 1968, Robert Tredgold described Bulawayo in the twenties and thirties as "a very good place to live," despite a shortage of water and roads that were "just dusty tracks." There were few cars, two movie theaters where films changed infrequently, simple amusements and sports such as rugby played on an "ungrassed" pitch. "We did not scorn to foregather of an evening to sing songs… or dance to a gramophone still in the development stage and requiring much laborious winding." Was this what Helen Odell had expected to find? Would she be charmed by this style of colonial life?

At least Helen finally received some mail from home. She was delighted to get a letter from her mother even though it had been written six weeks earlier. Letters from an old pal, Harry Babcock, and her friend Anne Dodge's husband would have brought her up-to-date on Stonington. However, no comment on Al's letter. She didn't even save it. But three days later she headed her diary entry with "Grand cable from Al." The cable read "MISS YOU GREATLY HAVE GRAND TIME BUT REMEMBER EMMETT FORGIVE MY DELINQUENCY ABOUT WRITING MUCH

LOVE, YOUR AL." I suppose 'Emmett' was some sort of private joke, which only adds to the intimacy of this telegram. He really did seem to be missing her, and small wonder she thought the cable was grand when she saw the way he signed it.

Helen then put her candid thoughts following a weekend in the bush into a letter to her sister:

Bulawayo
March 12th
Marje dear, Howdy stranger!

I last heard from you on Jan. 30th at Marseilles, France. I heard from Mother three days ago but it was written on the same day or a few days after yours. Well anyway, don't write here anymore. Write to Brown Shipley & Co. though I don't expect I'll stay in England more than a week. I don't know when I'm leaving here as all the ships are full. I'm on the waiting list for 3, ones the 13th, 20th, & 27th of April. I hope somebody will fall down & break a leg soon so I'll get it settled.

Bulawayo is a funny place, but I'm enjoying it. Lorna & Robbie are awfully nice – a little too nice for me I'm afraid, but it is good for me no doubt. They know all the 'best' people but really aren't interested & as far as I can see practically never go out or ask anyone here. I go marketing, etc. with her in the A.M. After lunch we sleep or read in bed until 4. Then have tea, then go for a little drive, then come back & have a hot gin & vermouth or whiskey & soda (one), then dinner, read & go to bed about ten. What they love is the veldt (open country). Every week-end they go off in the car.

We are just back to-day from an expedition. Mon Dieu, what an expedition. We went 75 miles to a ranch. I had the curse but I couldn't stay home because white women can't ever stay alone, not even in the daytime, so I had to go, but I wouldn't have if I'd known how bad it was going to be. We were on a road for about 40 miles. They said it was a road but I call it a corrugated cow path. We had lunch in some filthy hut where Robbie's uncle & family live. He was Prime Minister of Rhodesia, but it is not strange apparently that they live in what I call squalor on a farm now – people do very odd things here. Then we went on for 40 miles along dried up river beds, through fields of grass six feet deep, over rocks & hitting concealed ant hills 2 or 3 ft. high, through rivers (full) so the water was up over the floor boards & I don't know what. I had a tiny flask of gin & we got nothing to drink out there for the two days. It is a huge ranch, 250,000 acres, 15,000 head of cattle. Robbie's brother is secretary & assistant manager. Lorna & I slept in a sort of room & the 2 men, sister-in-law & baby slept on the verandah. We had no nets on our beds. The room was peopled with lizards, many huge spiders, one scorpion (killed by Robbie when discovered), a bat, 2 other weird birds & millions of mosquitoes & billions of ants. Robbie got ants in his bed so had to sit up the rest of the night. You can't get them out as they are in such droves. The privy was about ¼ mile from the house & was filled with all the aforementioned livestock as well as being guarded by snakes & jackals. Oh my – I much preferred the open spaces to the privy but there are too many natives lurking about so it isn't safe. On Sunday we had an all-day picnic! Then that drive back at night in a tropical rain storm. Robbie says often they get stuck in the rivers if there is rain & then that's that. You can't walk 50 or 60 miles to the nearest house. But we didn't stick, thank God! Today I have been & am still in bed for the day. Next week-end we go to visit people who have a feeble gold mine; they live in Kraals (mud huts with thatched roofs). Lorna told me reassuringly that they have some furniture or boxes that they use for furniture.

I wish you could see my clothes – the packing, public laundries, salt water, sudden rain storms, perspiration, moths, no places to hang or put things have certainly taken their toll. I'll have to have a whole new summer wardrobe when I get home. I'm certainly glad I didn't buy new ones to bring out here.

March 13th

Will just finish this off for the weekly mail. There is one in tomorrow & I do hope I'll hear from you. I trust you are well & having a good winter. All my love to you & Tom & the children.

Affectionately,
Helen

What a weekend! Rough and uncomfortable for Helen, who suffered from heavy menstrual periods and cramps, especially with scorpions and fire ants in the outhouse. Sporty was one thing, but this was just plain no fun for her. Aside from a few summer vacations in the Adirondacks, Helen had no experience of life without the comforts of beds and indoor plumbing. Wonder if she ever shared any of that little flask of gin.

Their first stop, the "filthy hut," did indeed belong to Robbie's uncle, his mother's brother, Howard Unwin Moffat, who had just finished serving as the second prime minister of Southern Rhodesia from 1927 until 1933. Howard Moffat was born at the Kuruman Mission in Bechuanaland in 1869. He was considered a Rhodesian pioneer and had fought in the second Matabele War as well as the Boer War. Later he oversaw the purchase of the country's mineral rights from the British South Africa Company. During his term, a Land Apportionment Act determining land allocation to white settlers was passed. This legislation still remains at the root of much of Zimbabwe's conflict today. The Moffats did build a very handsome small house in Bulawayo but perhaps not until after Helen's visit in '34.

Robbie's younger brother Alan apparently opted for the outdoor life, not studying at Oxford, but working in agriculture. He was, as Helen wrote, the assistant manager and secretary for one of Southern Rhodesia's big cattle ranches where he, his wife Zenith and baby Robin lived. Prior to the late 1960s Southern Rhodesian farms run by white settlers out produced those of any other African country and were able to export large quantities of food to the allies during World War II. Robbie's and Alan's older brother Jack had been killed in World War I. They also had two sisters, Helen and Barbara. When Robbie and Alan were very young, their father, Clarkson H. Tredgold, was appointed Southern Rhodesia's Attorney-General, and the family then moved to the capital, Salisbury. Robbie later graduated from Rondebosch Boys'

High School in Cape Town, South Africa. When he completed his education in England and returned to Southern Rhodesia, his father was serving as Chief Justice in Salisbury. In addition to practicing law in Bulawayo, Robbie also took on an additional job of acting judge for Northern Rhodesia in 1931. Helen had not only found herself in the midst of Africa but also in the midst of a very serious-minded colonial family.

Bulawayo
March 13
Dearest Mother,

I have just written Marjorie & Grandma but will dash off a line to you too to say hello & how are you. I get so tired of writing the same things over & over again and wish I could just sit down and relate to you the accounts of my doings. As a matter of fact by the time you get this I'll be nearly there to do it. I expect to leave here the middle or end of April, should get to England around the beginning of May & to America the middle of May – D. V. [Deo volente, God be willing] *Gosh, but it seems far and a terrific trek. I should not want to live out here & I don't think I'll be tempted as the few men I've met are not much to write home about, and there don't seem to be such droves of them as I have always been led to believe.*

I feel quite settled at Lorna's now & enjoying it thoroughly. We don't do much but are beginning to get dated up a bit now. Today we go out to tea & also to sundowners (drinks) & in the evening to a meeting. I don't know exactly what it is – it's called the Toc H – a partially religious & service club I believe & a result of the war. Next week I am speaking to them on 'America.' I don't know just what phase yet but will size them up tonight at this meeting & decide.

Lorna is fixing me up with golf & tennis partners so I can get some exercise. She doesn't play either herself.

I described to Marje my week-end on a ranch so won't go in to it again. She will give you the letter.

Kay Mason sent me a batch of Stonington Mirrors [newspapers]. Al sent me a cheery cable yesterday just as a greeting.

I do hope you are keeping well & not over-doing. You will be glad I imagine to get back to Stonington. It is the nicest & prettiest place I have seen anywhere yet & the most comfortable. Believe me I'll appreciate it when I get back, not that I haven't always felt the same about it. We are now going to have our morning tea so I'll stop.

All my love dearest,
Helen

Well, this letter seems to reveal the basis of Helen's desire to visit Africa. Tucked away in the back of her mind was the notion that 'droves' of eligible men might be waiting to greet her in Rhodesia. But that was turning out to not be the case. In many if not most instances, settlers had come out to Rhodesia to claim large pieces of land on offer, and they brought their new wives with them. This was especially true for the veterans of World War I in search of new and prosperous opportunities. One of the most vivid descriptions of the settlers' experience was provided by the writer Doris Lessing in her family story, *Under My Skin*. A later version of an English couple attempting to find the good life in Rhodesia is Alexandra Fuller's hair-raising memoir, *Don't Let's Go to the Dogs Tonight*. In any event, after just two weeks Helen decided that neither the local lifestyle nor the few eligible men appealed to her. However, as she mentioned, Lorna was making an effort to arrange some social events. That very afternoon, they went to tea at the home of Lady Russell, wife of Sir Fraser Russell. He also had been a chief justice and was about to be appointed acting Governor of Southern Rhodesia by the king of England in May of '34. Helen's diary entry regarding the tea: "too dull and funny!"

While doing morning errands with Lorna, Helen had visited every shipping office and travel agency available in Bulawayo. To her amazement, all the Union Castle ships were full returning to England even through April. She had assumed that since the trans-Atlantic ships were so affected by lack of travel resulting from the Depression, the same would be true for ships going to and from Africa. But there were far fewer Africa ships, basically only one line, and it was used by the Royal Mail, the British military, commercial interests, as well as general passengers. She even checked with Imperial Airways, the forerunner of BOAC and BA. In 1932 they had extended service to Bulawayo and South Africa. Helen then decided she would fly despite being "worried about the price." As an alternative to going by ship, flying seemed miraculously fast, nine days from Cape Town to London in 1934. Long distance Imperial planes could handle around twenty passengers, and they made stops along the way, only some being Salisbury,

Nairobi, Khartoum, Cairo, and Brindisi. Often the Italy-to-Paris leg was done by train. The plane ride was extremely bumpy, notoriously cold in unpressurized cabins, and extremely expensive. Nevertheless, she tried to reserve a seat. But on Friday, March 16th, after a session at the dentist, she "had a blow that all the planes are full. Went over all the damned ship business again. Hell."

Bulawayo
March 20th
Dearest Mother,

Am still here as you can see and expect I will be for probably another 10 days or two weeks, and then go to Cape Town. I am veritably a prisoner in the country as I thought for a while that I never would get passage on anything out. I decided to fly from Cape Town to London and thought it was all settled, then they said they were all filled up until the end of May, so I gave up that idea. I am on the waiting list for every ship & plane from April 10th thru May 10th. Then I remembered vaguely having heard at the Falls that they expected some 200 Americans in April from the 'Franconia.' I trekked all over Bulawayo the other A.M. & found that there was no agency here who had ever heard of the Cunard Line, let alone the 'Franconia,' no lists, no anything & no Cooks, so I wired to Cooks at Cape Town on Wed. & I got the answer this A.M. (Tuesday) saying the 'Franconia' is on a world cruise, leaves Cape Town on April 28th, arrives N.Y. May 30th via Montevideo, Santos, Rio, Barbados, & that they are reserving cabin E170 for me. So I guess I'll take it. It saves a lot of trouble not having to go to England & it would be nice to see South America. It will be a nuisance getting my money back from the Union Castle but can be done. It's the darnedest place to make arrangements from. If you write to Cape Town & post air mail Wed., you get the answer a week from Saturday at the earliest. I'd rather like to leave here soon but I can't afford to put in all the time until April 28th at hotels & in trains, things are too expensive. It will all work out somehow.

We spent last week-end at the gold mine. It was awfully interesting. It is a small mine but the workings & methods are just the same. Mr. & Mrs. Dye live in mud huts, all very crude but quite an experience for me. They are awfully nice & I enjoyed it. The place is about 50 miles away & in the leopard country. You can hear them often at night growling about. They keep about 5 big watch dogs to give the alarm & also to protect Mrs. Dye from the natives who often get quite wild & do terrible things. Lorna, Mrs. Dye & I slept in one hut on camp beds. The men slept in another hut on the mud floor. We ate at a table but sat on petrol boxes. We got up at six A.M. & went to bed at nine P.M. Yesterday A.M. we got up at 5:30 and motored back to town before breakfast. The roads were as unspeakable and as little like roads as last week!

Yesterday afternoon we went to a tennis party. It was exactly like England. I might just as well have been there. We have only been out twice in the evening since I came – once to a meeting of the Toc H., a sort of semi religious – social service & somewhat socialistic organization to which Lorna & Robbie belong & once to the movies to see "42nd Street" which I saw two years ago in America – so you see I'm not spending my life in great gaiety. [Actually, Helen had noted in her diary that the movie they had seen was

"Strange Interlude" with Norma Shearer and Clark Gable; she said it was unbelievably awful.] *Tonight I am speaking to the Toc H. on life in America! A big order.*

We only get mail once a week & tomorrow is the day so I am hoping for a letter from you all.

We never dress for dinner here, but after our siesta we bathe & change. Every day I wear the green silk (one of Mrs. Brady's) with the pleated skirt & brown embroidered squirrel on front or the yellow flowered silk made for me 3 years ago by Dassie. The rest of the day I wear cottons or linens & can only wear a dress one day as the heat & dust send it off quickly for the laundry. We have tea with boiled milk which makes me feel quite sick, at six A.M., for breakfast at 7:30 or 8, at 11:00 A.M., for lunch at 1:00, & again at 4:00 – 5 times. All the milk & water is boiled & we even have to brush our teeth in boiled water. I haven't seen any ice since I got here. I would sell my soul for a glass of iced water or iced tea. We don't eat any salads or uncooked vegetables, & we have corn on the cob (called mealies) for every meal.

I must stop now & go to town with Lorna.

All my love darling & thoughts & best wishes from Helen.

Picnic in the bush, March 11th.

The Dyes' "feeble" gold mine.

Kraals at the gold mine.

At least the weekend trip to the Dye's mine and mud huts met with Helen's approval, despite having to sit on petrol boxes. The privy was "lovely," and there was a gramophone for entertainment in the evening. She learned all about the mine and on Sunday morning accompanied the men to visit Old Mathieson, a prospector from as far back as 1880. She also helped look for some of the dogs who were missing. She loved dogs and would have been distressed if a leopard had gotten them. Earlier in the week Helen had gone with two of the Moffat girls and Lorna to see the ruins at Khami, (now a UNESCO World Heritage Site) just west of Bulawayo. These structures, dating back to the Torwa Dynasty of the Kingdom of Butua, were built before 1650 and were destroyed by the Ndebele in the 1800s. Additionally, Helen's Toc H talk on America had gone satisfactorily. So it seems that she was beginning to fit into the local life and was becoming more relaxed.

Nevertheless, after her talk on March 20th she wrote in her diary, "Lorna ill with fever. Think I'd better leave for many reasons."

Helen had told her mother about the telegram confirming her cabin on the Cunard liner *Franconia*, but didn't mention that she was going to wire Al back in Connecticut with an intriguing suggestion. Rather than return by ship via South America, she would try to get to Paris if he would meet her there. Sounds like a perfect scenario for a movie, another affair to remember. No doubt Helen thought the idea was romantic and adventurous, but how did it strike Al? Did she realize what a commitment it would have been? Al would have had to ask his brother-in-law for a very long vacation, book passage on a liner to France, the hotel, etc., in effect throw responsibility to the wind. And where would such an adventure lead? Al's recent memory of European travel also might have been a deciding factor. Three and a half years earlier his father had died unexpectedly on a trip to Europe with his new wife (Al's mother died of cancer in 1924). Al then had to travel to Switzerland to sign documents and accompany his stepmother, along with the body, home to Connecticut. But he must have been amused at the thought of such a rendezvous. His telegram, which didn't reach Helen until after she had left Bulawayo, let her down gently, "SORRY CANT MAKE PARIS WILL EXPECT YOU ON FRANCONIA TWO MONTHS SEEM AWFUL LONG MUCH LOVE AL."

With Lorna still ill and nothing to do but read, sleep, and drink tea, Helen made a plan to escape Bulawayo, "I shall leave on Monday before I go gaga from inactivity," she wrote. The one active highlight of the week was a brief game at the Bulawayo Golf

Club with a Mrs. Hobson. Helen saved her card showing that she shot a 46 for nine holes, except that they seem to have skipped the fifth. Not such terrific golf, but at least she was able to use those clubs that weighed on her luggage. The card indicates that the surface of the putting 'greens' was either sand or gravel and could be swept smooth only by the caddies. Helen reported that the caddies also carried little tin cups in which to wash the balls when they got covered with mud. According to the Local Rules, you were allowed to move your ball if it landed on hippo dung or fell into an ant or animal hole.

Helen's stay with the Tredgolds at 32 Borrow Street was passing the two week mark. Almost every evening after dinner Robbie, or 'Professor Tredgold' as she referred to him in her diary, would tutor her in Matabele and Rhodesian history while she took notes in a small journal. She instinctively knew how impossible it would be to remember it all. Even on her first night in Bulawayo Robbie had her reading a biography of Lord de Villiers (1842-1914), an esteemed chief justice of the Cape Colony and, later, the Union of South Africa. There was so much to learn about this unfamiliar continent – history, politics, native tribes, birds and animals, strange languages. For all Helen's complaints about dull evenings, her notebook reveals that she did begin to absorb scenes and impressions that were entirely unique to Africa. She noticed a "native poised on a kopje, looking for cattle" and that Lorna's "cook boy insisted on working on the floor because he didn't like tables." She noted the legend of the Honey birds who lead you to honey, but if you don't leave some for them, next time they lead you to a snake or evil spirit. She recorded that the rifle generally used for lions or leopards was a Mauser 9-3 or a 360, but that Robbie's was a 3-75. She also wrote that the "natives in Bulawayo must have passes (police) to go out."

Helen's final weekend excursion with the Tredgolds was a day trip to the Matopos Hills which she described in her diary.

> *Saturday, March 24. Helped with sandwiches, etc. & at 10:30 left for Matopos. Robbie very grim, dogs smelling. A lovely drive tho & the hills are really extraordinary. I was much impressed by the cave in Pomongwe. Then climbed the hill to Rhodes' grave. It is most impressive. Leander Storm Jameson & Sir Charles Coghlin (1st P. Minister) also buried there & the Shangani Memorial to Wilson & men who died in 1893 in Matabele War. The hills are scene of Rebellion in 1896. Lunch under a fig tree & I had a sun headache. Saw some klipspringer poised on a rock. Tea & home. Bed at 9. So gay it was!*

There is no way to tell what was making Robbie so grim. Could it have been the presence of an American houseguest for almost three weeks? A picnic at Matopos (now a UNESCO World Heritage Site known by its more precise native name Matobo) was a scenic and sensible choice. In his 1968 book, *The Rhodesia that was my Life*, Robbie called the Matopos Hills "our stamping ground ... a never-ending source of joy." Only about 20 miles southeast of Bulawayo, it covers an area of approximately 1,200 square miles and is made up of rolling granite hills sprinkled with very large boulders. There are also several caves, one being Pomongwe, containing ancient paintings and artifacts. Over the years Matopos has taken on sacred significance for natives and settlers alike. King Mziligazi, Lobengula's father, is buried there. The peace agreement that ended the final Matabele rebellion in 1897 was overseen by Cecil Rhodes in the Matopos Hills. His will reads, "I admire the grandeur and loneliness of the Matopos in Rhodesia and therefore I desire to be buried in the Matopos on the hill which I used to visit and which I called a 'View of the World,' in a square to be cut in the rock on the top of the hill…" When he died in 1902, Rhodes's body was carted to Matopos from Cape Town. Many believe that Lobengula was put to rest in the hills, and his sons definitely were. As Helen mentioned, Wilson, his men, and Jameson, all viewed by Zimbabweans today as brutal killers rather than heroes, are also buried there. Speaking at the site, in the presence of Queen Elizabeth in 1953, to commemorate the centenary of Rhodes's birth, Robert Tredgold drew attention to the graves of the "many good men, Boer and Briton, African and European, who, each in his humbler way, contributed to the building of our country." Nowadays, public opinion sees Cecil Rhodes and other colonialists in a very negative light as men who built countries to conform with their desires and prejudices, nothing humble about it.

Robbie and Lorna Tredgold seemed to have done everything in their power to accommodate Helen and proudly show her their country. It just wasn't the visit Helen thought it was going to be. She busied herself packing and shipped her trunks and bigger suitcases to Cape Town. She took more photos, one of a group of young native women who came by to sell "mud pots" and another of the three houseboys neatly turned out in their jackets.

However, it is impossible to tell if any of Helen's pictures are of Lorna or Robbie. There is one of his plucky 2-door Ford Sedan though. If my mother ever corresponded with them in later years, I was never aware of it, no blue airmail letters with exotic stamps, no Christmas photos from Africa.

Helen left the Tredgolds to a future fully immersed in Rhodesia. Robbie would soon be appointed Minister of Defense, responsible for the training of RAF pilots in the country during World War II as well as the controversial arming of native troops in the Rhodesian Africa Rifles regiment. In 1943 he was made a Judge of the High Court, in 1950 the country's Chief Justice, and in 1954 acting Governor-General for one year. Knighted in 1951, he was subsequently awarded KCMG (Knight Commander of the Order of St. Michael and St. George) in 1955. Robert Tredgold believed deeply in the nobility of England and the benefits of the colonial system. On the other hand, he understood the people of Southern Rhodesia and their need to determine their own future. His book, which was dedicated to Lorna, said it all, Rhodesia was his life. In it, he expressed in very frank terms the cruel realities of racial prejudice that he witnessed, and he accurately predicted the country's violent and discouraging future. In the end, his liberalism could not withstand the force of the conservative white minority. The government under Ian Smith declared independence from Britain in 1965. A 15-year long guerrilla war with black nationalists ensued until a peace was signed in 1980. From that time, Robert Mugabe and his ZANU PF party have been in control, responsible for the erosion of human rights and almost total destruction of the economy. Sir Robert and Lady Tredgold never did have any children, and Lorna died from cancer in 1972. Robbie went on to publish two more books about Africa, one on wild flowers with his new wife. He died in Rhodesia in 1977.

Lorna and Robbie Tredgold with the Queen Mother in 1957. (Photograph by R.D.K. Hadden, in The Rhodesia that was my Life by Sir Robert Tredgold, London, George Allen & Unwin, LTD., 1968)

Bulawayo
March 26th – Monday
Mother dear,

Just a hurried line as I leave in half an hour for Johannesburg & will be on the train until Wednesday afternoon & hence will miss the weekly mail both here & there. I just realized it. My visit

here is over. It has been most interesting & an unusual experience.
Not awfully gay however. So I'm not in tears at leaving. I feel as if I
had been to a school. I have learned so much history, geography, etc.
& in bed each night by ten & leading an exemplary life. Robbie is
extremely intelligent & has told me so much of the country's history
& development, etc. that my head is bursting with knowledge.

I set off now alone, knowing no one in Johannesburg & will
get caught there or somewhere over the four day Easter holiday!
However, maybe I can spend it on the train. I'll write you all about
it but must stop now.

All my love my darling,
Helen

At six o'clock, after a quick sundowner cocktail, Lorna and Robbie took Helen to the station. The three said their goodbyes, and Helen jumped on the train. As luck would have it, the Hillier-Holts, friends from the *Llangibby Castle*, were on the same train. She had dinner with them and then retired to her roomette, or coupe as it is known in South Africa, to read and sleep.

CHAPTER FOUR

South Africa

On the train the next morning, Helen was awakened at six with early coffee, instead of tea. She "shook the cinders off" and dressed. During the morning she quickly jotted down some sights in her journal: "native girls with bare bosoms; swarms of locusts; the sun turning white feathery grass to red; starving kaffir dogs; the light on the veld and distant hills." Later, when the train stopped at a small station, she bought two "funny wooden men and a basket from the natives." These two carved men stand shakily on my desk now, staring at me with wide-open round eyes. One is about 18 inches tall with an all-over burned black pattern on his skin and flat cap. He carries a long spear in one hand and a club in the other. He also has a distinguished pipe, but at this point it keeps falling out of the round hole which is his mouth. The smaller figure holds a spear and a shield, is decorated with a native chevron pattern, and has an upside-down bucket-shaped hat. The hat has a hole in the top, perhaps originally for feathers. His collar and small loincloth, made from very thin animal hide, are neatly tied around him.

I could imagine the train's interior compartments and dining car, Helen chatting with an English girl and the man in the next coupe – a Mr. Lance. But it wasn't until I read Nadine Gordimer's story, "The Train from Rhodesia", that I had a realistic picture of the exterior setting, "the squatting native vendors" and the train coming out of the horizon, "creaking, jerking, jostling, gasping," filling the station. Here Gordimer, who won the Nobel Prize in 1991 for her novels and stories portraying South Africa especially under apartheid, depicts white tourists haggling with the natives over their carvings, in this case a lion. I doubt Helen haggled much at all, but she still may have experienced the same remorse after the initial excitement of buying what she called funny men. "How will they look at home? Where will you put them? What will they mean away from the places you found them," Gordimer's young woman ponders. I know where my mother put these figures. They lay in the top drawer of a Queen Anne highboy in our front hall along with one or two other items from her African trip. They looked completely incongruous in our Connecticut colonial house. My brothers and I were allowed to peek at them occasionally, to know that our mother had once been to Africa.

Johannesburg
March 29th
Dearest Mother,

    It seems so funny to write the names of these places at the top of my letters. I can't believe I'm here, and yet on the other hand it becomes quite natural when one is here. If you see what I mean. As you know, I left Bulawayo on Monday & found the Hillier-Holts, from the Llangibby, *on the train. I also got to know a lone English girl and picked up the man in the next carriage to me, so I had a very social and pleasant trip – tho hot and dirty. The country was mostly flat veld and bush but the natives at the tiny stations where we stopped were interesting. They all come from apparently nowhere, to sell things. They are a funny looking lot – some practically naked, others with the most extraordinary costumes. One woman had on a black chiffon & sequin evening dress – very low cut (discarded of course by some white woman) over a ragged khaki man's shirt, thru the skirt one saw ragged calico just wrapped about her. In Southern Rhodesia I actually saw a man with a woman's old pair of corsets on him, up around his chest, the suspenders fastened across his shoulders for shoulder straps. You couldn't believe the things they put on, & the way they wear them.*

To continue with the trip – in the afternoon of the second day we stopped for an hour almost at Mafeking. It's a most disappointing sight – awful little town but of course interesting to feel you have been there. I got to Johannesburg at 5:30 A.M. & found the event of the year is on, the big Agricultural Fair & the town is seething. The hotel is packed & it's amazing I got a room at all. I must say it's not much of a room, small & no running water even in the room. This, mind you, is the roaring cosmopolitan Johannesburg and the Carlton hotel. There are only one or two rooms I believe with private baths. However, the visiting farmers & families are smart enough to raise the standard. Of course, only the rich ones stay here, and also out here farmers are of the upper classes, probably some are sons of earls or dukes, etc., for as you know many Englishmen have come out to try their hand. So, really some are most smart & attractive, others of course are very funny. I enjoy thoroughly watching them all. On Saturday I'm going to the Fair as I understand that's the best day. I'm also going out to see Robbie Tredgold's

117

sister who works in a native mission, & I am going to Pretoria, the capital of the Union, 35 miles from here. So, I'll be quite busy for the next three days. I am leaving on Sunday evening. I am going to Oudtshoorn & see some ostrich farms and caves, spend a night, then go on to George on the S. coast & go through what they call the garden route to Cape Town. It takes me at least a week to do it I believe. Cook's is arranging it for me. At Cape Town I shall stay at the Mt. Nelson Hotel for a short while. The Huttons are to be there too, then go out to Simons Town & stay at Lucy & Douglas' hotel until I sail. It's about one hour from Cape Town.

I am now definitely coming on the Franconia *having fixed it up this A.M. at Cook's here. The horrible cabin on E. deck below the kitchens, inside & no bathroom or toilet even on the deck, I turned down. Now they have had one cancellation but it's a double outside cabin with private bathroom on B. deck. I took it, having thought much & hard on it. So far I can't get on any Union Castle boats. Even if I did, by the time I got to England, shifted luggage & me about, hotels, trains, etc., it would easily cover the extra amount this cabin is costing me going direct to New York, and with it, I am seeing the three most important cities in So. America & a whole new country which I might never see again, having no friends or connections there. In fact, when I get home from this trip, it will take much to move me off again for a long time. Not that I'm not loving it all, but it is an effort, expensive & a wrench sort of to be so far from all the people one really cares about for so long. I would come home earlier in April if there were any way to do it, because one can really see as much of a place in a week as in three I think. I'm sure I could see all of Cape Town & vicinity in a week & I'll have to*

stay there three. The same in Bulawayo. I will have seen more in &
of Johannesburg in four days than most of the people who live here,
and from the trains, the veld looks all alike, in Northern Rhodesia
down through the Orange Free State, and all the stations look just
alike. There isn't anything like the diversity of scene as in America.
Imagine all the different things one sees there, say from New York
to Florida or from the East to the West coast where one gets moun-
tains, deserts, snow, tropics, plains & different characteristics in the
modes of living even. It hardly seems worthwhile here to go to places
as you know it will be so much like the last, except for a few instances
of course. This place is very different from Cape Town I believe. I
wanted to go to Kimberly, but everyone says it looks like every other
town so why go 700 miles to see it? So I'm not.

I was in luck here. I went to the [U.S.] consul's office in con-
nection with Norton Ritchey's movie business – and got nowhere
incidentally, but the wife of the consul-general, Mrs. Moorhead,
happened, unbeknownst to me, to be in the office & went down
in the lift with me. She turned & looked at me & said, "Are you
an American?" She was so nice & took me off with her in her car
for morning tea & asked me to their house for dinner last night.
I thought it too nice – never having even heard of me – I went &
enjoyed it thoroughly. It was a dinner in honour of the new German
consul & his wife. The Belgian & Portuguese consuls & wives
were there & an Austrian baron. It was most interesting. I talked
French all evening & was highly complimented on my fluency. We
played bridge some of the time, and I came home at one o'clock, I
being brought by the Belgians in their beautiful new Minerva [sim-
ilar to a Rolls Royce] *car which had just arrived from Belgium.*

Mrs. Moorhead says she'll call me up again so I hope to see her – anyway I'll leave cards before I leave. But wasn't it nice of her? It seemed so funny but so nice to see some Americans again.

Friday (Good)

I am being lazy this A.M. as I'm awaiting several telephone calls. I'm going to the Fair to-day as the Moorheads have invited me & will go to Pretoria tomorrow. She is going to ring me up about the time, etc. & Thomas Cook is ringing me up about all kinds of things.

Last evening I spent with a young German baron. I can't make him out exactly but he seems nice. He & I were about the only people in the hotel who are alone. All these Fair people know each other, so after staring at me all day Wed., the said German spoke to me yesterday, and after dinner last night joined me in the lounge & later we went to the cabaret in the grill. He is quiet & polite & intelligent but says nothing about himself. He travels for 10 months a year & lives in the country near Hamburg for 2. His mother and father are dead & he inherited the house but is too lonely to stay there for long he says. He is partly on a business trip according to him but he doesn't divulge his business. At tea time yesterday, the man from the train came in to see me. He is quite charming.

This letter is getting too long & heavy so I'll stop. I am thinking much of the approach of spring in Stonington and shall be sad to miss all of May there. I hope you can get someone to come & stay with you. I would certainly come earlier if I could. Well, my love,

before we know it we'll be together swapping experiences. Time goes
quickly after it has passed.

Affection & love,
Helen

Helen was overflowing with news and activities now that
she had reached the city of Johannesburg. Thomas Cook had
arranged for her to stay at the bustling Carlton Hotel, filled to
capacity with agricultural fair goers. The Carlton was opened in
1904, a crowning glory of the notorious Barney Barnato's building
spree. Barnato, who had made a fortune along with Rhodes creat-
ing the DeBeers Consolidated Mines, insisted upon all imported
furnishings for the hotel. The building covered one square block
in the center of Johannesburg and was renowned in its day as
a social and business hub but was torn down in 1964. And why
exactly had Helen been so disappointed in Mafeking? No doubt
due to her English heritage, she had heard stories of the valiant
British response to the gruesome siege there during the Boer
War. Commanded by Colonel Robert Baden-Powell (yes, founder
of the Scout Movement), the British along with many Setswana
natives held out for seven months, sustaining terrible depriva-
tions and casualties. In reality, Helen found the town devoid of
any heroic patriotic gloss. However, it was serving as the capital of
the Bechuanaland Protectorate despite being located just within
the South Africa border. Helen wrote her mother that everything
in Africa looked about the same, and one didn't need to spend
days traveling around and sightseeing. She must have just been

thinking of the scenery from the train, the straight tracks from Bulawayo through Bechuanaland and east toward Johannesburg. She must have been a little homesick for America as well. During my own travels in Africa, I was continually stunned by the variety of scenery, especially in South Africa. And as Helen went on, she realized that her first impressions were too hasty.

Helen had admitted to her mother that she knew no one in Johannesburg and would be all alone, but on her first morning there that all changed. While it was luck that put Mrs. Moorhead and Helen together in the same elevator, it was the consul's wife's discerning eye that recognized a rarity in Africa, another American woman. At that time, before globalization evened out fashion around the world, American style was distinctively casual to the point of being almost sporty. Helen was tall with long limbs, able to wear clothes with ease, and she exuded a natural alert look. Mrs. Moorhead seemed more than eager to meet someone from home, someone she could relate to. Her husband, Maxwell K. Moorhead, was the American consul general in Johannesburg from 1932 until 1938. Previously, he had been posted around the world from Belgrade to Rangoon to Stuttgart, thus she was well accustomed to diplomatic life. Muriel Moorhead was so delighted with her new American friend that she took Helen around with her all morning introducing her to several people and invited her for dinner that night. It seems that in 1934 just looking American could work wonders.

Helen also attracted the attention of a German baron, and he started talking to her as she sat alone having a sundowner in the Carlton lounge. That she mentioned this to her mother was surprising to me as my grandmother did not take kindly to Germans after having been a governess in Berlin in 1893, and then, of course, there was the Great War, not to mention the fact she was a teetotaler and might have disapproved of her unmarried daughter having a drink alone in a hotel lounge. I guess there were certain advantages in being so far away that you couldn't hear your parent's scolding. Mr. Lance, the man from the next compartment on the train, also appeared to be pursuing Helen. Back on the train, there had been an "awful fight" involving Mr. Hillier-Holt at dinner, and, whatever it was about, Helen felt sorry for his wife, having a "painful talk" with her the next day. Then, that telegram from Al, which had been forwarded from Bulawayo, saying he couldn't meet her in Paris caught up with her. Closing her diary on Thursday, March 29, Helen wrote, "All my men troubles are something!"

Helen may have been preoccupied with sorting out her "men troubles," but my attention was captured by the mysterious German baron and the new German consul at the Moorheads' dinner. After all, by March of 1934 Adolf Hitler had been chancellor of Germany for over a year, and his Nazis were the majority party. No one could have predicted the future then, but there were signs of trouble, even in South Africa. The connection between Germany and South Africa was strong at that time due to the fact neighboring South West Africa (now Namibia) had been a German colony and was then being administered by South Africa under a League of Nations mandate following World War I. It was understandable that the baron would have had business in the Johannesburg area or even in South West Africa. Germans had also traditionally supported the Boers, or Afrikaners, in their opposition to British dominance. But it was odd that the baron was not more forthcoming, and Helen sensed that.

Actually, an incident shortly before Helen's arrival in Johannesburg revealed how tense relations were becoming. Tucked into Helen's photo album were British newspaper clippings of Prince George, the Prince of Wales' youngest brother (later the Duke of Kent), on a tour of South Africa in February and March. An internet search revealed that while Johannesburg was preparing for the royal visit, flags from many countries, including Germany's swastika flag, were hung from the post office building. Protests were made, especially by Jews, and city officials had the swastika flag removed. At that point, the German consul immediately registered his protest, but the flag remained down. Was this then the new German consul that the Moorheads entertained a little over two weeks later? Was Helen, with her acceptable conversational French, added to the party in order to defuse any strained relations? It turned out that due to intense threats, the South African government was compelled to ban the Nazi party in South West Africa later that year, but pro-Nazi activity continued in South Africa itself.

Carlton Hotel
Johannesburg
Good Friday [March 30]
Dearest Marje,

Have written to Mother to-day but feel like writing to you too, or starting to, as it is time I got dressed for dinner. I have just been to

the great yearly exhibition with the Moorheads, the U.S. Consul &
wife. It was most entertaining, everything there – new motor cars,
practically all American; bulls; chickens; pigs; industrial exhibits;
horse races & jumping; etc. People come from all over southern
Africa to attend, many of them camping out. The 'rich' ones stay
here. Johannesburg is a smaller, unfinished what – certainly not
Paris – maybe Detroit would be nearer to it. The city is crowded and
noisy beyond words, but outside are the most beautiful houses with
gorgeous gardens & swimming pools, etc. It is barely 50 years old.
They say even the dust in the gutters has some gold in it. People have
made money quickly but apparently spend it too. It is also very cos-
mopolitan. I have met loads of Americans & there are many French,
Germans, Belgians, etc. I am quite fascinated by it & hate to leave.
Of course I was so lucky in meeting the Moorheads. They couldn't
be nicer, much older than I but simple, friendly & gay Americans
with no affectation. I met Mrs. Moorhead in a lift & she takes me
off in her car with her & introduces me to people, asks me to dinner
at her house. If I were Roosevelt's daughter or her favorite niece, she
couldn't do more. To-night they are dining here at the hotel with the
wife of the President of Pretoria University & she has fixed it with
her for me to dine & go to the movies with them!

After the exhibition to-day we had tea at the country club, a most
attractive place, low & rambling & tables on the lawn. Several other
people joined us. There is an 18-hole golf course & a 9-hole & 20
tennis courts. They say they have wonderful dances there, and the
people are terribly attractive looking. I had to buy two dresses yesterday.
I thought I'd sightsee & go to bed at nine while here. I literally knew
no one, so brought one suitcase & dressing case, & shipped the rest

to Cape Town. I thought for once, and being alone, I'd travel unhampered by my usual amount of luggage. And I get into this. As most of my clothes are on their last legs anyway, I really need the clothes & had planned to buy something in Cape Town so might as well do it here. I got a blue & white striped wash silk dress & an evening dress with silk coat. It is white with large blue dots, the coat blue but lined with same. It probably sounds funny but is really quite smart. I was lucky to find them as I had all blue shoes, accessories, etc. with me for my other things. I travel always in blue & white print (bought in Nassau, made by Dassie) with navy blue linen jacket. In Bulawayo I wore my coolest clothes – tennis dresses, etc. It is cooler here as I wear Margaretta's brown & white; blue suit with foulard blouse (Bergdorf) & various silk dresses or would had I brought them. I only brought Westerly [Rhode Island] *blue chiffon dinner dress with sleeves which is dropping apart, & Westerly black chiffon for evening, also dropping apart. I left for rummage sale in Bulawayo three straw hats beyond repair & too old fashioned, the yellow print made by Dassie & one pair of worn out shoes. More will be abandoned later...*

Helen must have had to change her clothes for dinner as she left off the letter to her sister at this point. She described the Johannesburg Country Club in such glowing terms, just the sort of place she loved and perhaps had expected in Bulawayo. Clearly, she was having a better time now. Her diary reports that she dined with Mr. and Mrs. du Toit along with the Moorheads, and they all went off to see the British comedienne, Cicely Courtneidge, probably in the film *Falling for You*. A. E. du Toit was vice-Chancellor and Principal of Pretoria University from 1927 until later in 1934.

Over the next two days Helen made the most of her time in Johannesburg. On Saturday, she took herself off by bus to sightsee in Pretoria, visiting Paul Kruger's house and lunching at the stylish Polley's Hotel. Back at the Carlton that evening, Hinrich, the German baron, joined her for dinner, and afterwards they "walked, then went to the cabaret and had a swell time, dancing and discussing Germany. Bar closed but he had his own plans." I'm sure he did have his own plans, but what about that discussion of Germany? Time and history can rearrange things, putting a new slant on subjects. Today it's hard to even imagine them having a "swell time" dancing while talking about Nazi Germany. In the spring of 1934 the heavy weight of that conversation didn't really exist, or at least it didn't exist for these two people. They seemed to be happy to enjoy a few days, much like a fleeting shipboard romance, without looking too far into the future. The following day, Easter Sunday, Helen wrote that she "got up feeling not too well but I went to the Cathedral all alone." She lunched with Hinrich at the hotel. It was her last day in Johannesburg, and she boarded a night train "almost in tears at leaving all my nice friends and a German!"

The second part of her letter to Marje was written on Tuesday, April 3rd, in Oudtshoorn.

Have just had a bath & then lunch, having arrived here at noon. I left Joburg on Sunday evening & am supposedly on my way to Cape Town. I don't know just why I'm in Oudtshoorn, or exactly where & what it is, but everybody told me to get off here & see it, so I did. From what I've seen so far I'd like to leave tomorrow, but I find there is no train tomorrow unless there are enough cattle going out, then there'll be a freight train. People here travel all the time on freight trains but it's one thing I haven't done as yet. The passenger trains are bad enough when you get off the main route. Last night there was no diner but they gave us ½ hour – 4:45-5:15 – to get food in a station. I wish you could have tasted it – pork & onions I believe it was, with fried potatoes & mealies at quarter to five too! I haven't had a drink of water since Sunday. It isn't safe to drink any water anywhere, & they don't sell any bottled water except soda. I nearly die of thirst & now I find one can't drink it here either. I probably won't have any till I get to Cape Town on Saturday or Sunday.

I hated to leave Joburg. I had a beau there – a German named Hinrich, very nice. He took me to the cabaret on Saturday night & I had a grand time. He is coming to Cape Town next week so I hope to see him there. He also saw me off on the train & took me to lunch on Sunday. Sunday afternoon the Moorheads took me for a drive & to the club for sundowners (drinks). They also came to the train & also the Belgian Consul & wife. It's a great custom here, if you like someone, to see them off. It's quite a social gathering, the platforms packed with people bearing flowers, etc. as the trains only go once or twice a week it makes them much more important. I also went to a tea on Sunday to meet Mr. Fourie who is the Minister of the Interior, & he was on my train the first day. He had me paged & asked me to lunch with him in the diner. He gave me a letter to a man here who has an ostrich farm & in 15 minutes I am setting out to find him, as I can't locate him on the phone. Mr. Fourie also gave me a letter to a man in George (my next stop), & when I get

to Cape Town I'm to meet Mrs. Fourie. I made many friends on the
train including two killing English women tourists who are staying
here, so I have someone to speak to here.

One has to go to one's room after lunch in this country, so as
there is never a desk or ink, I am using the pencil. There also is no
chair in the room so I am sprawled on the bed. The writing hence is
not of the best I know.

I'm anxious to get to Cape Town to see if I have any mail as I
have had none now for two weeks. Drink some water for me.

All my love,
Helen

Doesn't know why she's in Oudtshoorn or where it is. Helen sounds like your average exhausted tourist continuing on in a daze toward the end of a long trip. It had taken her over a day and a half on two trains to travel more than 600 miles from Johannesburg down to Oudtshoorn in the Little Karoo area of the Western Cape. She wasn't thrilled with the train's "dirty old bedding" or the station's pork and onion supper (which today's traveling gourmets might tout as interesting ethnic cuisine). Nevertheless, Thomas Cook had booked her into the Queen's Hotel, even now an elegant smaller version of the Victoria Falls Hotel. Oudtshoorn ("a place with a most uncomfortably Dutch name" according to Anthony Trollope in 1877) was, and still is, known for ostrich farms. It experienced a boom economy in the late Victorian and the Edwardian eras when ostrich feathers were the rage in ladies' hats, fans, etc. The town is also a short distance from the Cango Caves, a twisted series of spectacular caverns, featuring dramatic stalagmites and stalactites, in the limestone at the base of the Swartberg Mountains. Presumably, Oudtshoorn had been recommended for these attractions.

Queen's Hotel
Oudtshoorn
April 5
Mother dear,

I've had the most amusing time here. It is a small village or town, about the size of Mystic, but the hotel is quite nice. One gets to know everyone in the hotel right away. The first night an English woman was put at my table. She is a great character. She works her way about the world, was in New York for two years, saved enough money to come here; has been here four years. I don't know where she will go when she leaves here. She is in the real estate business in Cape Town but is now on a holiday all alone in her baby Austin, a very risky business going about alone out here & everyone is horrified. She asked me to go out to the caves with her yesterday so I was delighted. She wore khaki shorts & looked too funny. As usual the road was horrible & we bounced and banged about. The caves are so big, it took over two hours to go through them & I was nearly dead from the climbing and crawling and the air. It was an amusing expedition though. I had tea with the Misses Neville, two funny English tourists, and at dinner two very attractive girls were put at my table & we all went off to the movies, about a four-year-old picture of New York black-mailers.

This hotel is absolutely full. I am leaving at noon for George, but as I hear there is a mayor's conference there & every room in town is taken, I don't know what will happen. There is not a train from there to Cape Town until Saturday. It is certainly a new experience for me traveling in a country like this. When I get to Cape Town my traveling will be over except to get me on the ship.

I am definitely coming on the Franconia, *arriving New York on May 30th or 31st. Don't try to meet me unless you really want to. Al said something about meeting me but by that time he may not want to or be able to. However you might ring him up & find out if you want to. If he or you or Marje or anyone meets me, they better bring some cash with them, not that I've bought anything, but I may be broke by then & need train fare. Won't I be glad to see you!! But what a trip I will have had. Mon dieu, all over the world I've been, it seems. I can't believe that I'm going to see some of South America too. I'm glad about that as I doubt if I'd ever really set out to go there from home & yet I would love to see it. I met 3 people in Joburg going on the* Franconia, *so I set out knowing someone already. I must pack now to go to George.*

All my love dearest,
Helen

When I first read this letter, I wondered if George was another man that Helen planned to rendezvous with, but soon realized that George is a town located about 30 miles south of Oudtshoorn. It is a commercial center for what is known as South Africa's Garden Route, an area stretching from Mossel Bay east along the Indian Ocean coast past Plettenberg Bay. With the mountains on one side and the beaches on the other, the Garden Route has always been a very popular tourist destination. Helen's journey to George on the train would have taken her over the Outeniqua Mountains. The spectacular rail route, with its seven tunnels and multiple switchbacks, was built in 1908 and more or less parallels the 1847 Montagu Pass, still considered one of the world's most dangerous roads. Despite the slim chance of getting a room in George, Helen plowed on with her Thomas Cook itinerary.

Monday, April 9th
Mt. Nelson Hotel, Cape Town
Mother dear,

I wrote you from Oudtshoorn but didn't mail it as there was no outgoing mail. Now I am in Cape Town. After leaving Oudtshoorn I took the train to George and such a ride through the gorgeous mountainous country. I was really frightened to look out of the window, but it was <u>beautiful</u>. As I feared, I couldn't get in the hotel at George, so took a bus that runs on rail tracks to Knysna. It took two hours & a half to get there, but that too was magnificent scenery. I was so tired when I got there at 7, in time for dinner, and I took a violent dislike to the hotel. It was very common, dismal and I hated it. I spent the night however, by necessity. At 6:30 the next morning, however, I arose and left on the 8 o'clock bus and went to Wilderness, a place near George of which I had heard much. It is <u>beautiful</u>, right on the sea with huge mountains behind, and an <u>excellent</u> hotel. I got there in time for lunch, then after a rest I played golf. A man was starting out alone too & we played together & had a grand time.

He joined me that evening after dinner & introduced me to everyone in the hotel, & I had a merry evening. The next morning I played in a gold foursome, 3 men & I. After lunch I left and hated to go but had made my plans. I went into George in a car with 5 men from the hotel also going on the train to Cape Town. The train was packed, in three sections, each one about a mile long. I was in a carriage with two fat women, both Afrikaners but very nice, but it was awful getting undressed, etc. and the train was utterly filthy.

I got to Cape Town yesterday (Sunday) at 12 noon. I came to the Mt. Nelson Hotel & have a nice room & <u>bathroom</u>. It is a nice hotel, the only good one here, set in lovely gardens, but about 2 miles from town so one has to go on the train or walk which is quite a nuisance. It is <u>terribly</u> expensive, 35 shillings a day. The Huttons are here & I sit at their table in the dining room. It is fun being with them again. John McCormack (the singer) & also John R. Mott are both staying here, but I haven't seen them yet. They just arrived on a ship this A.M.

Lucy rang me up today. She is coming in town tomorrow to lunch with me & I am going back with her to some cocktail party & dinner. They can't get in their house for a month and are at a hotel. I think I'll go out there next week & stay until I sail, as it will be cheaper & I'd like to be with Lucy. Also the Huttons leave Friday & it will be dull for me here. Simons Town, where Lucy is, is about a forty minute run on the train from here.

This A.M. I went to the museum but this afternoon I am resting as tomorrow will be strenuous. I have some letters [of introduction] *to people but will wait for a day or two until I feel better to use them. I found my luggage here alright, it having taken two weeks to get here by freight from Bulawayo. I also found two letters from you. I am so glad you went to Nassau, and do hope you enjoyed it. I am having so much glorious sunshine that I am glad to think of you having some too. I wish I could describe the flowers and the colors and lights & shades out here. I can't even attempt to half tell you about any of it in a letter, but I'll have enough to talk about when I get home to last me for the rest of my life. What a trip! I like it all better all the time and am just beginning really to take it in and get a sense of perspective on it. Bulawayo is about the ugliest & drabbest place out here, but since then I have been dumbfounded by the country.*

Mother dear, I am sorry though not to get home before the end of May. It rather weighs on my conscience to leave you for so long. But honestly, I've been working ever since I landed on my passage home. No way that I could come even if I got accommodation, which I can't, would get me there before the end of May, so it's unavoidable. You won't believe it, but people are booking now on ships for next Christmas to go to England. They get their leave every so many years, and they know exactly when it will be & they book nine months ahead. Even at this hotel, they turned dozens of people away this morning as three ships came & it's full.

I wonder how my rock garden is faring. Do tell me if my dogwood trees bloom this year and which plants come up. But no – you won't be writing any more after you get this, unless you write to Rio de Janeiro or Barbados. I don't know when we get there.

I'm crazy to hear about Nassau and who you see, etc. I hope the filthy old Munson boats won't sink with you on board. They are terrible old tubs. I went last year over to Miami on one of them. I'm so glad your blood pressure is lower, it's a great relief to hear that.

Kay Mason sent me some more Stonington Mirrors & some Smith Alumnae News & I was delighted to get them.

Please excuse the pencil. There is never a desk or ink in the rooms.

All my love, dearest. Keep well,

Helen

Helen was getting to be an old hand at coping with the vagaries of traveling in South Africa. She recorded that there was an "extraordinary Boer family" on the "bus" that ran on the rail tracks eastward from George to Knysna, an oxcart waiting for them when they arrived. The next morning, she abandoned Knysna and the unsatisfactory hotel, taking the bus back along the coast to another resort called Wilderness. This so-called bus was most likely a small local steam train with bus-like coaches. Known as the Outeniqua Choo-Tjoe, it only stopped running in 2007 due to flood damage on the tracks. Luckily, Helen found an attractive hotel in Wilderness which offered golf. She elaborated on the afternoon there in her diary. "Tea & a Mr. Leggat (78) picked me up & we played golf together. It was great fun & he very good. Had several sundowners together & he told me of his engagement to Miss Evans. I laughed & it was true. After dinner he told me about the ring, then introduced me to the Ogilvies & some other right nice people & we had a good evening." The following day Helen played in that foursome with "old Leggat" along with Mr. Ogilvie and another man. She then had to take the bus back to George to get the regular train to Cape Town. Several men were also on the same bus and the train, notably a big man who was helpful and provided a bit of comic relief during the "horrible, hectic dinner."

And so, finally, on April 8th Helen reached Cape Town. It made sense that Thomas Cook had booked her into the Mt. Nelson Hotel as it was owned by the Union Castle Line. She was delighted to rendezvous with Jack and Susan Hutton, friends from the *Llangibby Castle* who had also been at the Victoria Falls Hotel with her. The history of the Mt. Nelson Hotel mirrors the history of Cape Town itself. The Dutch initially settled the Cape in the mid-1600s as a supply port for Dutch East India Company ships. The hotel property, which is on a slope at the base of Table Mountain, was granted to the Dutch governor in 1743 for purposes of farming. However, in 1806 the British permanently took over Cape Town, and the farm was renamed for the hero of Trafalgar, Lord Horatio Nelson. New owners then planted beautiful English gardens there. Sir Donald Currie, owner of the Union Castle Line, purchased the property in 1890 in order to build a 'splendid' hotel for his passengers. The Mt. Nelson opened in 1899 and has hosted luminaries such as Winston Churchill, the Prince of Wales, and Oprah Winfrey over the years.

In 2011 my traveling companions and I walked through the imposing entrance colonnade to the five-star Mt. Nelson and up the steep palm tree lined driveway, the rambling big hotel spread out to the right. Since the 1920s the buildings have all been painted 'Mt. Nelson Blush,' a light pink reminiscent of Bermuda or Nassau. Helen was right, the hotel is about a two-mile walk from the center of Cape Town. We had strolled the length of Government Avenue, past Archbishop Tutu's St. George's

Cathedral, the Houses of Parliament, and what is left of the Dutch Company's Gardens, now a park that ironically hosts a full-size statue of Cecil Rhodes pointing north toward his Cape-to-Cairo vision, erected in 1908, although recently attacked and in danger of being removed. Helen was also accurate in writing that the Mt. Nelson was expensive. Thirty-five shillings in 1934 would have been about $8.75, or slightly over $205 today. Actually, these days you would be lucky to get a comparable room there for less than $500 a night, only breakfast included.

The first thing that greeted us upon walking into the hotel was an array of vintage Union Castle Mail Steamship posters that decorated the walls of the reception area. I recognized instantly how proud of that connection the hotel still is despite the fact that it is now owned by Belmond Ltd., formerly Orient-Express. The sumptuous, and famous, Mt. Nelson afternoon tea was going on when we arrived, and the lounge was packed with a multi-racial group of ladies in hats, children in party dresses, and a few gentlemen in suits. Fully booked, we were told by two very handsome young head waiters in well-fitted poplin suits. They encouraged us to sit outside on the pleasant verandah overlooking the gardens and order whatever we desired from the bar. When I told these maître d's why I was so interested in the hotel, they were amazed and promptly pointed out the Sheraton-style dining table, laden with cakes and canapes, as well as several hotel-silver pastry servers that had all come from Union Castle ships. I silently toasted my mother while I sipped a glass of rose wine on the verandah.

*The verandah at the Mount Nelson Hotel,
Cape Town, 2011. (author photo)*

*Union Castle Line poster in the reception area of
the Mount Nelson Hotel. (author photo)*

The Mt. Nelson Hotel was home to Helen for a little more than a week. She enjoyed sightseeing around Cape Town with the Huttons, visiting the museum to see the bush men dioramas as well as the snake park and the waterfront. Of course, she didn't have as much sightseeing to do as tourists today. No tour of the bleak Robben Island where political prisoners, including Nelson Mandela, were held from 1961 to 1991. No visit to the District Six Museum to see the pain caused by forced "urban renewal." Back in Johannesburg, Helen wasn't offered a tour of the Soweto Township, nor was the Apartheid Museum there to overwhelm her with history of that brutal period. All that loomed in South Africa's future.

One day Helen and her friend, Lucy Ross, sat on deck chairs in the hotel's garden and later had lunch with the Huttons. Lucy, her two small daughters, and her husband Douglas, a British naval officer, had only recently arrived on a ship from England. As Helen told her mother, the Rosses were stationed in Simon's Town, where the British Navy was based. They were living in a hotel there until their house was ready. Simon's Town is halfway down the Cape of Good Hope Peninsula on the False Bay (eastern) coast, about 24 miles from the center of Cape Town. Helen was then invited to drive with the Rosses out to Simons Town for a cocktail party and to spend the night at their hotel. Confusingly, it was the Lord Nelson Inn, an all-together different experience, far smaller and much more casual than the Mt. Nelson. The inn is, still today, situated along the main road and faces the harbor. The next morning Helen looked after the Rosses' daughter Daphne on the nearby beach. Back at the hotel in Cape Town later that day, she had a surprise visit from Mr. Leggat, the gentleman golfer from Wilderness.

April 14, Saturday
Mount Nelson Hotel
Cape Town
Mother dear,

As I am busy all day tomorrow and on Monday, I shall write you tonight for the weekly mail which closes Monday night. Pretty soon there will be no use my writing as you won't get it before you get me.

I have been here one week tomorrow and have enjoyed it in many ways, in almost all ways, but I am most anxious to leave and be on my way home. The next two weeks will seem very long I'm afraid. The past week, of course, the Huttons were here & I enjoyed being with them, but they sailed yesterday. I went down to see them off on the Warwick Castle. *They have had their cabin since last November and I believe the U. C. Line now when they said they couldn't take me. I've never seen such crowds in my life. She sailed at 4 P.M., and I came back here & had a solitary tea and dinner & went to bed at nine o'clock & read. Today I have been on the rush. I have to get a Brazilian & Argentine visa on my passport and what a business I've never seen! I have to have 3 photos each for them; a vaccination certificate which thank heavens I have from Dr. Halliday; a health certificate! I spent one hour this A.M. in a doctor's office & then he couldn't see me so I have to go back on Monday. They take your fingerprints too, then soak you 5 pounds*

for Argentina & 3 pounds for Brazil. I am almost busted now &
have given up tea & drinks. I never take a taxi & we are 2 miles
from town at this hotel. I walk or go in the tram. With care I think
I'll just make New York.

This afternoon a Mrs. de Villiers, introduced by Mrs. Moorhead
of Joburg by letter, took me to the races. Great fun but I lost 10s.
Tomorrow she is taking me for a drive around the peninsula (saves
me £2/10) & I go there after to a dinner party. (Saves me nothing
as the terms are inclusive here & I'll have to ask her for tea.) In the
morning my German beau is coming to call! He sails on Monday &
only got here tonight from Johannesburg. On Monday I go to Simons
Town for a week. You can stay at the hotel there for a week for the price
of one night here. But after a week there is no more room so I have to
go somewhere from Monday till Sat. when I sail. There is nowhere in
Cape Town but here so I don't know what I'll do. I have to leave my
luggage here & my mail comes here. Dr. Mott says I must come back
here as it's the only respectable place! I introduced myself to him &
have been talking to him all evening. He talked much of Father &
remembers him well. It got me all upset & quite homesick. He (Dr.
Mott) is a grim man – he never smiles or looks at you – he's all mis-
sions and uplift in a dreary efficient way. This hotel, as well as being
expensive, is grim and dreary too – just like the Union Castle line
who owns & runs it. There is no one under 90 and only about five
of them & no one speaks to each other. They are all English except
Dr. Mott & me. And the food is awful. Cape Town is disappointing
to me – beautiful setting and scenery but the town is smoky & dirty
and shoddy & ugly & hot (just now anyway). I expected it to be so
beautiful that I guess I expected too much. I've had a lot of surprises

on this trip – hardly anything has been the way I expected it to be – some things better and some things worse. It is autumn of course and the rains are expected but haven't come. There is a hot monsoon all the time & every one is nervy. I feel so tired all the time, everyone does, especially after coming from a high altitude as I have. I have been to the museum & to the snake park and to see some old Dutch houses and the zoo & university & to Rhodes' Memorial.

And how was Nassau? I do hope you had a nice time and feel well after it. It's a funny little place, but nice I think. Stonington is nice too & the spring will be coming along now. How topsy-turvy. Winter beginning here & summer there. How lucky I am to have a home I love so. I pity desperately the derelicts floating about out here in the hotels, always seeking a better place. I feebly suggest that they settle somewhere and start some roots, but they don't seem to understand. I have talked to many of them.

I must go to bed. I'll write again next week & then no more I imagine, although I won't be home for a month after that. All my love darling. Cheerio. Happy days. Happy birthday tho late.

Aff. Helen

Helen was in a gloomy mood now that her friends, the Huttons, had sailed off on the *Warwick Castle*. "Felt as if I were saying goodbye to a half of me," she wrote in her diary. She even saved a lengthy article from *The Cape Times* describing the 20,000-ton ship's departure, "a notable event in dockland." In the last paragraph the writer was able to capture the emotional wrench that British colonials experienced seeing their colleagues off.

"The cheering broke out with renewed vigour, handkerchiefs were waved, the very last good-byes were said, and the maze of coloured streamers broke one by one as the ship was taken out and turned for the entrance, carrying 640 holiday-makers to enjoy a sea voyage under ideal conditions in the finest month of the year, and who are the envy of all those who were compelled to stay behind, but who look forward with hope that the day will come when they too are numbered among the fortunate ones."

Chatting that evening with Dr. Mott didn't do much to cheer Helen up. "Grim, never smiles or looks at you...all missions and uplift in a dreary efficient way." What a description of the man who had been the general-secretary of the International Y.M.C.A. for thirteen years and was currently the president of the Y.M.C.A. World Committee. Helen's father, Joseph H. Odell, had known John R. Mott for many years and considered him "the most constructive religious genius since John Wesley." The two men had corresponded together about missions in Asia, and in 1911 Odell had written a profile of Mott for *The Outlook* magazine. When the United States entered World War I, Mott headed up the Y.M.C.A.'s vital support of American and French troops, an effort similar to that of the USO during World War II. Joseph Odell, as a special correspondent for *The Outlook*, traveled to France in 1918 to report on the work of the Y.M.C.A. and wrote about Mott's leadership. Obviously, Helen found it difficult to share her father's profound admiration for Dr. Mott. Conversing with him just caused her to feel sad and far from home. (In 1946, John R. Mott would be awarded the Nobel Peace Prize, shared with the international peace advocate Emily Greene Balch.)

Helen had to kill two more weeks in the Cape Town area before boarding the ship for South America for home. But lucky for her, a generous and hospitable woman arrived on the scene to save her from social boredom. Mrs. Moorhead, the U.S. Consul's wife in Johannesburg, had written asking her friend, a Mrs. de Villiers, to look up Helen at the Mt. Nelson Hotel, and she did exactly that. But who was this Mrs. de Villiers? Helen neglected to record details, however with a few clues in her letters and diaries as well as some internet research, I was able to find the most logical candidate. Adelheid Selma Hélène Koch was born in 1889 in the Province of Natal (now KwaZulu-Natal). In 1911 she married Charles Percy de Villiers, the son of South Africa's chief justice, John Henry de Villiers, the very same Lord de Villiers that Robbie Tredgold had Helen reading about on her first evening in Bulawayo. The de Villiers family was descended from early Huguenot settlers, and John Henry had been honored with knighthood, the K.C.M.G., and a new title, 1st Baron de Villiers of Wynberg, primarily for his work in the Transvaal at the conclusion of the Boer War. After he died in 1914, the title of baron naturally passed to his oldest son Charles. Helen only mentioned Mrs. de Villiers, which makes sense as the 2nd Baron died on February 10, 1934, at the age of 62, only slightly more than two months earlier. Perhaps Mrs. Moorhead wanted to provide Mrs. de Villiers, just 45 years old, with a diverting assignment – entertain this nice young American woman.

Lord Nelson Hotel
Simon's Town, C. P.
Wed. April 18th
Mother dear,

I moved out here on Monday, just bringing some hand luggage, and leaving my trunks in town. Simon's Town is one hour on the electric train from Cape Town. It is much nicer being here with Lucy & Douglas than all alone in town and much cheaper. I wrote to you I believe on Saturday night. On Sunday Hinrich Postel, the German, came to see me in the morning & we had lunch together. Then right after lunch Mrs. de Villiers came for me and took me for a perfectly beautiful drive around the peninsula. It is magnificent scenery. We ended up at her house for tea. It is a farm, grapes for wine. The house is an old Dutch house, built in 1685, and is perfectly lovely both inside and out. We had tea & Mr. John Watt came, an old gentleman whom I had met with the Huttons. Then I changed, having brought evening clothes in a little bag, and for dinner arrived Mr. & Mrs. Linnell (the U. S. Consul), Dr. Hamman (German Consul), a Mrs. Mackenzie & another (South African) & a Col. Kupper (another German). It was a lovely dinner and we played bridge afterwards. Dr. Hamman brought me back to the hotel [the Mt. Nelson in Cape Town]. *It was a very pleasant day, and being Sunday, might have been a very dull & dreary one so I was fortunate. On Monday morning I had my health examination & you'll be glad to know that I have no trachoma, tuberculosis or syphilis. I also packed & in the afternoon moved out here. I have a very nice room & the food is good but there is no place to sit. The hotel is right on the street & very noisy, no garden or anything, and it is unbearably hot. It gets this way apparently before the rains set in.*

Yesterday I had to go in town again as I was invited to the House of Parliament to a luncheon by Mr. Fourie, the Minister of Labour. His wife was there, an Italian woman, another man & another American Consul. It was very interesting. I met Gen. Smuts and Prime Minister Herzog. Mrs. Fourie & I went into the gallery & listened to the debates until about half past three. Then I took the train to Rondebosch & had tea with Sir Clarkson & Lady Tredgold (Robbie's mother & father) & I got back here at seven exhausted. Today I've been just milling about here recuperating.

Friday, April 20th

Darling, it is your birthday and I have been thinking about it all day – and for many days past actually. I was _so_ angry and still am. Last Monday I went to the Post Office & sent you a cable – deferred rate – telling you I was sailing definitely on the Franconia and wishing you a happy birthday. The next day they rang me up to say that there was no such person as Odell in Stonington, _Illinois_. It cost 17s & I had the worst row with them. They said they had fulfilled their contract. I took the matter to the U. S. Consul & he is still working on it. I am absolutely in the right but it's hard to work on a gov. thing like a post office. In the meanwhile they still insist there is no Stonington, _Conn_ & won't accept another cable there. I'll send you one as soon as I can.

Saturday, 21st

I dined last night at the U. S. Consul's, Mr. & Mrs. Linnell, whom I met at Mrs. de Villiers' last week. The Norwegian Consul and wife were there, the daughter of the German charge d'affaires, the Swiss Consul & wife, the Belgian Consul & the U. S. Vice-Consul. It was an awfully nice party, I enjoyed it no end. A naval man, Commander Webber, who lives here was dining in Cape Town so he took me, and stopped and brought me back, otherwise Heaven knows how I would have got there.

In a few minutes I am going to a tennis party, then a cocktail party & then a dinner party. Next week is getting all booked up with things and a week from today I sail.

I suppose you are back from Nassau by now & in Stonington. I certainly feel far away at times – my goodness – and I get about one letter a week, none from you for about three as I suppose your Nassau trip made a delay in letters.

Simons Town is a funny little place and I am wondering how Lucy will like it for two & a half years. Most people do like it I believe. Her house is very nice and there is a little beach for the children nearby. She has about ten callers a day and everyone is very cordial and friendly.

I must stop now. All my love, Mother darling. I hope you are well and enjoying being back in your own home once more with the oriole, and wrens and robins. We all come running back in the spring.

Cheers & God bless you,
Helen

P.S. I can stay here until I sail after all and am so glad.

Helen just kept the letter to her mother running along like a diary, filled with the frustrations of communication and the details of a very busy social schedule. Might as well, since letters only went out about once a week. She did not tell her mother that her Sunday meeting with Hinrich was "strange and fantastic," perhaps because she realized that she would most likely never see him again. The tantrum over a 17 shilling telegram was, I imagine, misplaced homesickness, but oh, what minutia consular officers have to deal with!

Once you have driven around the Cape Peninsula, you realize what an incredible tour Mrs. de Villiers gave Helen on that Sunday afternoon. "Perfectly beautiful" hardly does it justice; stunning and breathtaking are more like it. The diary mentions Chapman's Peak road, which is carved into mountains high above the rocky Atlantic coastline south of Hout Bay. It's not clear whether they went as far as the Cape of Good Hope Point before turning up the False Bay coast, but their drive must have been long and scenic. (One wonders, did Mrs. de Villiers, herself, drive or did she have a chauffeur?) Finally, they reached the de Villiers' farm, described by Helen as a lovely old Dutch house with a wine cellar, built in 1685. This could describe several estates in the Cape area, many with vineyards. However, I came across the de Villiers name in a large, illustrated book of South African colonial houses published in 1988. That house, and farm, Rustenberg, is situated in Ida's Valley, 5 kilometers northeast of Stellenbosch, the center of the country's original wine region. It dates back to 1683 and seems the most likely candidate for Mrs. de Villiers' estate.

According to Graham Viney, author of *Colonial Houses of South Africa*, Charles Percy de Villiers purchased the Rustenberg estate sometime between 1904 (the death of the previous owner, Charlotte Merriman Barry) and 1914, when he became the 2nd Baron, probably just after his marriage in 1911. In addition to vineyards, the farm raised cattle and produced prize-winning fruit for the London market. The house and outbuildings have been remodeled and added onto over the centuries, but still maintain their elegance and simplicity. Photos in Viney's book show the exposed ceiling beams and wide-board floor of the main house's deep central room. Nearby there is a 150 foot long stepped-gabled wine cellar building. Although Rustenberg is quite a distance from the center of Cape Town and the peninsula, it seems to fit Helen's description of Mrs. de Villiers "perfectly lovely" house. Today Rustenberg is a beautiful vineyard open to the public. Of course, I had to go there, but, alas, the main house and its grounds are out of sight and kept private, its garden open only one day a year. However, I was able to enjoy a tour of the winery buildings, another spectacular garden, and, naturally, a delicious wine tasting.

*Building at the Rustenberg Vineyard, typical of
Dutch Cape architecture. (author photo)*

Once more, Helen seems to have been swept up in the diplomatic crowd at Mrs. de Villiers' dinner party. And again, Germans figured prominently. The United States consul at the time was Irving N. Linnell, a Harvard Law School graduate who had also served in London and Ottawa. (In 1939, Linnell, as consul general in Prague, was able to provide the State Department with intelligence on the Nazi invasion of Czechoslovakia.) The Linnells followed up by inviting Helen to their dinner party five days later at their house in Wynberg, a suburb of Cape Town. Perhaps she enjoyed that evening so much because, as she wrote in her diary, it included "dancing and carpet golf." After the party at Rustenberg, Helen revealed in her diary that Dr. Hamman, the German consul, "brought me home and scared me." That would have been 35 miles of anxiety all the way back to the Mt. Nelson in Cape Town.

When I read the paragraph in Helen's letter about her visit to Parliament with Cabinet Member A. J. P. Fourie and his wife, I was amazed. Imagine meeting Prime Minister Barry Herzog and Deputy Prime Minister Jan Smuts, former Boer generals and long-time leaders of South Africa, names out of history books. Adriaan Fourie, whom Helen had met in Johannesburg and lunched with on the train, promised to introduce her to his wife in Cape Town. Fourie, who was actually Minister of Mines and Industry, had been in politics and government for many years and served earlier as Cape administrator in the Herzog government. After taking turns as prime minister from 1919 to 1933, Herzog, with his National Party, and Smuts, along with the South Africa Party, had recently formed a coalition government. However, as the twentieth century proceeded, these three men would play pivotal roles leading to the South African policy known as apartheid, which the National Party brutally enforced from 1948 until 1994. Somehow, through a chance meeting in an elevator, my mother, traveling alone in a very distant country, met various dignitaries, visited the South Africa Parliament, listened to speeches, and ended up shaking hands with these heads of the government, men who had and would continue to impact world events. Not your run-of-the-mill tour by any means.

Simons Town
April 22nd
Marje dear,

Your two letters of this week were very welcome — more than you can probably ever imagine unless you one day find yourself alone in

South Africa. Also I was so enchanted with Henry's [Marje's son] *poem of the sea. I felt moved as you did by it. How I would love to see him, all of you in fact. Another five or six weeks seems an eternity until I do – although I am loving my visit here and consider it all well worth visiting, and myself the luckiest person imaginable to have had such a trip. I can never explain or describe it to you, I'm afraid, but it is filled with so much of interest in beauty and experiences of all sorts, some pleasant and some wearying but all different.*

At the moment I am living the life of the [British] *Navy. It too is certainly unique in many ways, although sometimes it is so familiar that I marvel that I am away off at the ends of the world. This hotel is small, crude but clean and friendly and adequate. I eat with Lucy & Douglas & do everything with them & they are so nice. I am devoted to the children too. Then there is another life – two other naval officers & wives living here and four other naval bachelors – it is as though we were all just living in one private house. We play tennis & golf and go to the same cocktail parties, etc. Last night we went to a "Wilson Smith" party – all games and organized, etc. I also have launched forth on my own in government circles, as you will hear from my letter to Mother and have lunched at the House of Parliament & met the Prime Minister and other ministers and dined with various consuls. My name has been in the paper several times as a <u>distinguished</u> over-seas visitor, but unfortunately I forgot to cut them out as proof of the "success"! I did cut out today, though, the enclosed clippings re the Franconia. Can you believe that my old flame of Troy adolescent days, Eugene O'Brien, is to be my ship mate for a month? I really am thrilled about the trip back via So. America & on the luxury liner. I never* *have seen or heard so much about a ship. People almost beg to touch me when I say I am going on the* Franconia. *It is considered the peak of all luxury and everything wonderful – lectures every day by Hendrick van Loon, current event lectures by a Mr. Batchelder; French classes, bridge classes, 2 tennis courts, 2 squash courts, an out-of-door theatre, 2 London surgeons & a N.Y. dentist, movies, more well-known titles & celebrities than on any other cruise & je ne sais quoi! I may say I am paying for it, but what else could I do when everything else was filled up, & to wait here & go via England would have easily consumed the difference. So Alibi Helen argues, but for once or maybe twice I think it is true.*

We've had such a beautiful drive today to the tip end of the cape – the Indian Ocean on one side & the Atlantic on the other. It was gorgeous. We had a picnic tea & I did enjoy it. I have only five more days here and I am filling them up to the brim with trips and parties. I am going to Rhodes' home tomorrow & later out on the Dorsetshire, the flagship of the fleet. On Tuesday in town on business & to a luncheon at Wynberg (a suburb of Cape Town) & back to a dinner here. On Wed. I'm playing golf with a Commander Webber & lunching also at Wynberg & so on through until Saturday when I sail for Buenos Aires, Rio, etc. & HOME. Stupid letter this, but there's so much to say I can't say anything.

No end of love.

As Helen told her mother and sister, the social life in Simon's Town was busy, almost breathless. Her diary entry for Saturday, April 21 reads, "Over to the [new] house to plant more seeds. To morning tea at Mrs. McKenzie's. The Barnards came for drinks. Lunch & to the club for tennis with Ravenhills & Mrs. Pelley & Dr. Patrick. Tea there. Back & changed & to the Lethbridge's to cocktail party. Talked to many people & Mr. Harvie. Dinner & dressed & to party at Montgomery's. All kinds of appalling games. Taylor Young very helpful. Awfully tired." Of course, this social life was in complete contrast with Helen's stay in Bulawayo, and while she enjoyed the whirl, the essence of Africa had more or less disappeared. She became caught up in the British colonial lifestyle and was finding it slightly exhausting.

The main street of Simon's Town, South Africa, in 1934.

The Lord Nelson Hotel in Simon's Town, 1934.

Helen finished the week by playing golf with the "amusing" Commander Webber, inviting Mrs. de Villiers for dinner and bridge at the Lord Nelson Hotel – "poor meal but she very nice" – and taking in a rowing regatta between crews from the three British ships in port. Helen and Lucy even made time to see Maurice Chevalier and Jeanette McDonald in the 1932 film 'Love Me Tonight.' In the middle of the week, Helen took an early train up to Cape Town to finalize her arrangements. At Thomas Cook she was "soaked" another ten pounds. Annoying errands included stops at the Argentine and Brazilian consulates and then the Mt. Nelson Hotel to label her luggage and change her clothes. Finally, she took a train and taxi to the suburb of Newlands to have lunch with Mr. Watt and Mrs. de Villiers. The train back to Simon's Town stopped at the town of Fish Hoek for some reason, and she ended up walking about three miles the rest of the way. On her last full day in Africa, she played golf again with Commander Webber at

the venerable Royal Cape Golf Club and "beat him pathetically."
Her evening featured a cocktail party on the HMS *Carlisle*.

HMS. Carlisle, *where Helen attended a cocktail party on her last full day in Africa. (postcard)*

April 26th
Dearest Mother,

 Whether you will get this before you get me, I don't know but I'll send you a line anyway. Day after tomorrow I sail! And I am quite ready. A little more than ready actually. Of course even when I get on board I have another whole month but even so. I'm on my way and moving slowly homewards, and I must admit the trip on this cruise of the "luxury liner" Franconia intrigues me. I had no idea when I booked that I was getting on such a renowned cruise. I am starting off knowing several people & with introductions to many more. One man in Cape

Town was told yesterday by someone here to look me up & he said he was tired of me before he met me as he had five cards with my name on them from five different people telling him to look me up. He is a well know surgeon here with a stupid wife, I understand. Douglas Ross knows the Captain – they were together in the Dardanelles during the war & when they come to see me off, hope to see him & introduce us, etc.

Life here in Simons Town is very pleasant, somewhat like it is in Stonington. This A.M. there were crew races from the various ships & everyone turned out to cheer. There is a small club somewhat like ours, where everyone meets & plays tennis & has tea in a simple but friendly way. There are many cocktail parties, and some very simple parties of an evening, also some very formal ones at the Admiral's. This hotel is somewhat like the Carnarvon Arms, Dulverton, only not as good, and it is noisy as it's on the main street. But there are several naval couples here, and about six officers alone. We all know each other and it's quite cheery. I have been playing golf several times with one very nice commander. I know everyone here almost as well as Lucy & Douglas as I have been here almost as long.

April 28th

I was interrupted the other day, and now am in a great rush with my packing to do, etc. Right after lunch Lucy & Douglas take me in town to the Franconia. Several other people are coming to see me off too, at five we sail.

Au revoir darling. I hope the ship will go fast.

Love & kisses,
Helen

Luxury liner – the alliterative phrase was as sleek as the Cunard Line's RMS *Franconia* itself. Six hundred and twenty-three feet in length, the *Franconia* was launched in late 1922 primarily to cater to wealthy passengers. While the liner crossed the Atlantic back and forth between Liverpool and New York during the summers, she was famous for the southern hemisphere cruise around the world during the winter and spring. And luxury was certainly an apt word to describe her interiors. From the article in the April 24th *Cape Times* newspaper that Helen sent to her sister, we know that the *Franconia* had an indoor pool with teak paneled walls decorated with bronze friezes copied from Greek vases, a squash court, garden lounges filled with pots of evergreens and palms, and a card room decorated like "an old Georgian club in St. James." Most impressive seemed to be the smoking room which resembled an English inn complete with a brick fireplace and stained-glass windows. The liner was built to accommodate at least 1,700 passengers in first, second and third classes, but only carried around 300 or so when cruising, all first class, with a crew of more than 433. As the *Cape Times* pointed out, "the traveler today requires a steady and spacious ship, he also demands variety, interest and activity, and healthy occupation for enforced leisure." Most of the passengers had been enjoying their "enforced leisure" since leaving New York on January 9th as well as extensive shore excursions and sight-seeing all arranged by Thomas Cook at each port. The passenger list noted those travelers who left the cruise or embarked along the way. Helen had already put exotic Africa far behind her and could endure some leisure provided she was cruising toward New York, but this voyage wasn't going to be strictly transportation like that on the *Llangibby Castle*. It held the promise of much more pleasure.

Lucy and Douglas did take Helen up to the ship in Cape Town on the 28th, stopping on the way to tour Groote Schoor, Cecil Rhodes's house, for one last bit of African history. The C47 cabin with adjoining bath was "very nice, but not extraordinary... very comfortable." Although there wasn't much of a party, Mrs. de Villiers and her friend John Watt showed up for a bon voyage cup of tea before the *Franconia* sailed at 5 o'clock. Helen wrote, "The Rosses left & I waved good-bye until last sight & we sailed out of Cape Town for home." Later, in the dining room she discovered that she was seated at the doctor's table.

CHAPTER FIVE

On Board the RMS *Franconia*

A s the 'luxury liner' *Franconia* set out on its 3,657 nautical mile journey west across the South Atlantic, Helen slept comfortably in her cabin, relieved to be on the last leg of her trip. Waking up on Sunday morning, she decided to take advantage of all that the ship had to offer. Enjoying breakfast in bed was first on the list, followed by attending a church service, then securing her assigned deck chair and settling into it. Later it was tea, an invitation to cocktails, and a concert by the ship's orchestra in the evening after dinner.

As the week progressed she went to several teas, one given in her honor by the Social Directress Miss Boyer, and, of course, more cocktail parties. A couple from Norwalk, Connecticut, who had been on the around-the-world cruise the entire time along with their young son, gave a cocktail party for Helen on Thursday to introduce her. Unlike the *Llangibby Castle* passengers, most on the *Franconia* were Americans returning to New York. During the day she usually played deck tennis (somewhat like volleyball only played by tossing and catching a rubber ring rather than a ball). By Friday, Helen was in the deck tennis tournament but lost in the semi-finals on Saturday. She also lost a ping-pong match. However, not deterred, she participated in those two other cruise ship rituals, "horse races" and tango lessons.

A lecture by Hendrik Willem Van Loon took up Monday evening, and Helen found it "quite entertaining." The Cunard Line had hired Van Loon, a 52-year-old scholar, popular writer and world traveler, as guest lecturer for the entire journey. Van Loon was born in the Netherlands but came to the United States to study at Cornell University. He went on to obtain a Ph.D. from the University of Munich and returned to the states after the First World War to become a citizen. By the time he embarked on this world cruise, he had written and published at least 24 books and articles, actually only about half of his lifetime work. Many of his books were histories aimed at young readers, but adults found him engaging as well, and he usually illustrated his books with his own art work. In describing Van Loon, critics all seemed to agree that he was 'exuberant' and 'larger-than-life.' Traveling with him was his wife, Mrs. Van Loon, at least that is how she was listed among the passengers. Eliza Helen Criswell was his second wife, but Van Loon had divorced her in 1927 in order to marry for the third time. Obviously, that marriage did not last long as Eliza Helen, or "Jimmie" as she was sometimes known, accompanied him on the *Franconia* in 1934. It has never been clear whether they were officially remarried. On Tuesday, cruise staff member Charles Batchelder gave a talk on the up-coming ports-of-call, Montevideo and Buenos Aires. Batchelder later delivered a Dictatorship Lecture Series, one talk on Mussolini, another asking "Has Hitler Saved Germany?" and a third on Stalin. Judging from Helen's diary, she skipped all three.

Cunard liner RMS Franconia, *painted white*
for Southern Hemisphere cruises.

May 6th I think
Mother dear,

    You will have had to adjust your mind to thinking of me now in
mid-South Atlantic instead of North. They seem to look just alike.
Day after tomorrow we get to Montevideo at about 6 P.M. then we
go on a river steamer up to Buenos Aires and arrive there on Wed.
morning early. We have all that day and Thursday there, then come
back on Thursday night & have all day Friday to see Montevideo.
    This really is a wonderful cruise. There are some awfully nice
people, and as there is no 2nd or 3rd class, there is lots of room
to spread out & you never feel that people are on top of you. The
cabin & food seem the height of what they should be after the food

163

& quarters I've had most of the time for the last four months. Miss Boyer, the hostess, gave a tea for me the second day out & a man at my table asked me to a cocktail party that night, so between the two I met lots of people & now, I believe, know everyone and feel perfectly at home. It certainly is different from the old Llangibby. *There are many deck sports & a lovely pool. Hendrik Van Loon gives a lecture every now & then on South America, also a Mr. Batchelder gives illustrated lectures on what we are going to see, and on current events. There are French lessons & contract bridge but I haven't gone in for those. I take tango lessons tho in a class. It is really remarkably well run and even the people who have been on for nearly five months don't seem to be tired of it. Which is pretty* [good] *proof of its success. I sit at the Doctor's table. He is most attractive, very clever I believe, with an extraordinary record in research work for the Rockefeller Foundation. He was badly banged up in the war & had to give up & come to sea for his health. The* Mauretania *is his ship really but they took him away just for this cruise. There are three other women & 2 other men at the table & it's quite amusing.*

As I will be home so shortly after this letter & as air mail is very expensive, I won't write more. I can hardly imagine what it will be like to be at home again. I've tried to put it out of my mind in order to get the most out of my trip but soon I'll luxuriate in thinking of my homecoming. I hope you're well, darling.

So much love.

And so ends the last of Helen's letters to her mother. Any more would never reach Connecticut before her own arrival. Thus, as she had not gotten any letters from home in a very long time, she found herself completely on her own, quite dependent on making new friends with people who had been happily cruising around the southern hemisphere for four months.

Dining table assignments in the luxury liner heyday carried a lot of weight. These were the first passengers one would get to know well. These were the passengers with whom one would spend the most time, every meal. Helen listed her tablemates in her diary, "Miss Duerr & funny old Miss James, a Mr. H. [from] Australia, Mrs. Wilson & Mr. Draper." She seemed quite taken with the head of her table, the ship's surgeon, even telling her mother a bit about the man. But writing in her diary after the first day at sea, she confessed, "Dr. Carr is a most extraordinary man, the kind I'm quite unable to cope with." Nevertheless she ended up in his cabin later that evening after the concert, having a drink along with another passenger, Roland King. To be clear, the doctor's cabin was probably more like a small suite, suitable for entertaining. As the first week progressed, Helen spent more time with Dr. Carr and Mr. King, retreating to the doctor's cabin after almost every lunch and dinner, usually in the company of others as well. She mentioned him frequently in her diary, sometimes by his initials G. C. and, by the time she wrote her mother, using his nickname Bill. However, none of this excluded socializing with other passengers, specifically Larry, Marshall, Jan, and Carl, and having "a grand time" spending an evening dancing.

George Jameson-Carr had been working as a doctor, or surgeon as the British say, on Cunard Line ships since 1921. He was originally from Edinburgh, Scotland, the son of a Presbyterian minister. Maybe he and Helen talked about their fathers and the ministry. In any event, Bill, as he was known to friends, received his medical degree from Edinburgh University in 1910. He had then gone to the Amazon region working to help eradicate yellow fever, which is perhaps where the Rockefeller Foundation came into play. He served in World War I, recovered from his wounds, and then decided to become a ship's surgeon. By the spring of 1934 he was 49 years-old, seventeen years older than Helen, and acknowledged to be tall, handsome and worldly. The question remains what was it about this man that Helen found so difficult to cope with? On May 8, after ten days at sea, the *Franconia* arrived in the harbor at Montevideo, Uruguay, and at 10 P.M. passengers were scheduled to board a river boat for the overnight trip up the Rio de la Plata to Buenos Aires. Helen wrote, "Bill took me over to the river boat & saw me off & introduced me to some people. So sweet."

*Dr. George (Bill) Jameson-Carr at his table
in the* **Franconia** *dining room.*

The Thomas Cook-arranged Buenos Aires excursion sounds like a typical optional cruise tour – overnight on the river boat going and coming, meals, one night at the luxurious new Hotel Continental in Buenos Aires, drives around the city stopping at every notable building and statue, etc. The all-inclusive charge was $68. Helen felt a little under-the-weather on the first morning but struggled through the afternoon drive with a Mrs. Murray. The following morning she went on another city tour, in her opinion "terrible, so silly except for the opera house," which would have been the still-renowned Colon Theatre. For her, the tour's highlight was Thursday afternoon's real horse races at the Jockey Club's Argentino track. "Great fun. Won some money." She finished the day with Mati tea in a gourd, drinks and dinner at the hotel and an amusing movie before getting back on the river boat at 11 P.M. The following morning Helen, accompanied by a Mr. Schultz, toured Montevideo by car, but when she returned to the *Franconia*, she was unable to see Dr. Carr as he was busy making arrangements for a passenger who had died during the night.

As the *Franconia* continued north along the coast of Brazil, Helen resumed her shipboard social life – drinks before lunch with friends, cocktail parties before dinner, bridge games, and tango lessons. Her friend Roland had made several purchases while ashore and presented her with a puzzle ring. She had lunch at Dr. Carr's table as usual and dropped by his cabin afterward. On Saturday evening she gave a "very funny" little cocktail party. The Van Loons showed up although she hadn't invited them, and a Mrs. Bennett entirely forgot to come. To make up, the Van Loons invited Helen to dine with them that night, and Hendrik presented her with two hand-colored sketches that he did on the back of the menus, one presumably of the table setting, the other a caricature of a large man in a raincoat, most likely Van Loon himself, walking a toy dog. Helen also saved a menu from the following evening with another Van Loon sketch depicting a scene from Dante's Inferno, Canto 17, showing Virgil pointing to the third species of sinners, the Usurers, surrounded by flames. Van Loon included his own dramatic caption, "Beware of these my child, For they are wicked folks." Judging from the wide variety of gourmet offerings on the menus, dinners must have been delectable and quite lengthy.

Hendrik Van Loon sketch of a man walking a dog.

Hendrik Van Loon sketch of the dinner table on the **Franconia.**

When the ship docked in Santos, Brazil, on the morning of May 14, passengers boarded a special train taking them on the scenic three-hour journey inland to Sao Paulo. Dr. Carr was able to get the time off and so joined Helen and Roland. They all had lunch at a hotel, toured the city by car, and returned to the ship in Santos. The following morning they found themselves in Rio de Janeiro for the first of three days in that famously exciting city. On her first excursion, Helen "went up Sugar Loaf though utterly petrified." She and a friend named Eva lunched at the Copacabana Palace Hotel and enjoyed a drive around the city and the Botanical Gardens. She pronounced Rio a "marvelous city." But, at this point Helen's diary takes on a moody tone. "Back & drinks with Charles, Malcolm & others. Dinner & so tired & tired of everybody."

There was one person who was really getting on Helen's nerves. In her diary she called him "Imp," and as often as I try to figure out who he may be, his identity remains a mystery. In São Paulo, "Imp most annoying." The first day in Rio, "Imp so excited over Rio – impossible." The prime candidate for Imp has to be Dr. Carr, but somehow the behavior seems inconsistent with his background. Of course, Imp could also be Roland or her old friend Eugene O'Brien or some other unnamed fellow. On the second morning in Rio, Helen didn't even show up for the Corcovado excursion. "Was so depressed I thought I'd die – gave R.K. an awful shock, poor man. I was in a state." Now, this sounds serious, more than just being worn out with traveling. After dragging herself out on the afternoon excursion to the Tijuca Forest, she wrote, "Back & saw Imp for a minute & then he came & fixed things & I felt better." Suddenly, life looked far rosier, depression lifted like an early morning fog, and the day finished on a high note. "Went to the Hotel Gloria for dinner with Roland & to the Copacabana after. Met Bill there. He danced with me. Won at Roulette. Eva joined us & it was a swell evening."

The last day in Rio was a whirlwind. Helen, joined by a Mrs. Rusterholtz, began it with a game of golf at the spectacular Gavea Club overlooking the ocean. Her diary breathlessly sketches the rest of the day. "Rushed back to Gloria Hotel and met Bill, Roland, Eugene O'Brien, Carpenters, etc., drinks, then grand lunch with Bill. Such fun. Back to ship and flew in a plane all over Rio. Marvelous. Back & watched us sail out. Such a night and such a city!! After dinner spent evening with the Imp." Oh no! The Imp is back, but not to worry. Mercifully, this seems to be the last mention of that name. Incidentally, later in her life, Helen was always afraid of flying, so nervous that she usually took half a tranquilizer pill just before take-off and a stiff drink during a flight. She blamed her fear on a topsy-turvy landing at the end of this Brazilian plane ride but, curiously, makes no mention of it here.

Leaving Rio, the *Franconia* passengers settled in for another week of games and partying while the ship made its way north to the Caribbean island of Barbados. Helen's days were filled with swimming, deck tennis, and drinks with a variety of passengers including the Van Loons, a woman nicknamed "Stackie," and a Mr. McAlpin who had come onboard in Montevideo. But, as she wrote, "life getting complicated." It seems that Roland was making a play for her, but she was more interested in Bill's attention. Meanwhile things were "strained" at the dining table because "funny, old" Miss James was "green with jealousy" and "absolutely on her ear about me." This presumably because Dr. Carr was indeed paying attention to Helen.

The relationship between Helen and Bill was flourishing, and they were spending every evening together. They usually had cocktails before dinner with a group of friends. After dinner, the doctor may have had to see patients, but, apparently, his time was his own after 10:00 p.m., although one evening they went to a movie at 8:45. Bill consistently earned Helen's code-like diary comment of "too sweet." On Tuesday, they went down to the tourist deck bar and had hot dogs and coffee. For some reason, this novelty was memorable, "I shall never forget it – never." I doubt it was the hot dogs that she would always remember. For a more surprising bit of intimacy, the doctor did Helen the favor of removing moles from her nose and neck, assisted by the chaplain on Wednesday. On Friday, she met him after Van Loon's lecture and found herself "up in the bow after with him. Gorgeous night. Very late had coffee & biscuits in his cabin." This was all sounding too much like the famous scene in the movie "Titanic." Where was this shipboard romance heading? Obviously not toward any icebergs, but still I needed to learn more about Dr. Carr.

A simple internet search for George Jameson-Carr revealed far more than I expected, starting with photos of him surrounded by reporters and continuing on to the Wikipedia page, "The Death of Starr Faithfull," among countless other entries. Considered one of "the World's Greatest Unsolved Crimes," the disappearance and subsequent drowning of the beautiful 25 year-old Starr Faithfull is a long and sensational story. It took place in 1931, exactly three years prior to Helen's trip on the *Franconia*. Carr had been acquainted with the young woman and offered himself as a material witness in the investigation of her death, which explains the mob of reporters. Much to my relief, he had not been a suspect. Newspapers across the country carried the story for months. *Time* magazine even chimed in with one of their typically saucy items, "The Press: Five Starr Faithfull."[1] How could Helen Odell not have known about it? Didn't someone on the *Franconia* whisper about it? If she knew, she might not have wanted to alarm her mother in a letter, but wouldn't she have noted Dr. Carr's connection to the lurid story in her diary?

---

[1] "The Press: Five Starr Faithfull", Time, June 29, 1931.

Dr. Carr encountered Starr Faithfull for the first time in June of 1927 on Cunard's *Aurania* shortly after leaving Montreal, bound for England. He had been summoned to a third-class cabin by the nurse to deal with a comatose young woman and her intoxicated lover. Later, when asked if his relationship with Starr had been romantic, he replied snappishly, "You don't become romantic about a girl on whom you used a stomach-pump the first time you saw her."[2] During the *Aurania* crossing, Dr. Carr was summoned on several occasions to try to subdue Miss Faithfull who had been drinking and was becoming hysterical, insulting passengers, and generally causing problems. During the voyage he gained her confidence and learned about traumatic experiences of sex abuse in her past, as well as her repeated use of drugs and ether. Quite naturally, she later took to writing letters, some "charming and amusing,"[3] to the doctor, and he, in turn, tried to steer her toward getting a job as a writer. In August of 1928 Starr showed up intoxicated on the *Aquitania*, after it had docked in New York, looking for Dr. Carr. Later that year, she sneaked onto the *Laconia* in Liverpool and conned Dr. Carr into guaranteeing her passage back to New York or she would jump overboard. (Her well-connected, but perpetually short-of-funds, mother and step-father never reimbursed Carr.) She continued to show up regularly at bon voyage parties, overindulge in alcohol and drugs, and inevitably succumb to prurient relationships.

---

[2] Goodman, Jonathan (1996) The Passing of Starr Faithfull. Kent, Ohio: Kent State University Press. p.212.

[3] Ibid. p. 214.

On Friday, May 29, 1931, Starr sought out Dr. Carr at a bon voyage party on the *Franconia*. However, by this time the doctor was on to her schemes. He rejected her, telling her to get off the ship as it was about to sail, but she remained on board. In the nick of time she was discovered and forcibly removed to a tugboat as the ship steamed out of New York Harbor. The following week was a blur of her heavy drinking, visits to ocean liners, and hotel stays with assorted men. Finally, on Monday, June 8, her body was discovered washed up on Long Beach, Long Island. Despite an exhaustive investigation, it has never been determined whether she committed suicide or was assaulted and thrown into the water. In any event, Dr. Carr, crossing the Atlantic, had a perfect alibi. Upon arriving in England and hearing the news, he returned immediately to New York on the *Laconia* in order to testify. He produced three letters that Starr sent to him during her last week, professing her love for him and threatening to kill herself, as proof of her unstable mental condition. By this time, the story of Starr Faithfull may be sounding familiar to readers. In 1935 John O'Hara couldn't resist borrowing it to create Gloria Wandrous in *Butterfield 8*. The alluring female passenger, the doctor, and demon drugs also play their twisted parts in Katherine Anne Porter's *Ship of Fools*. In other words, the story was well-known, but not worthy of a mention by Helen Odell.

But enough of Bill Carr's past. Helen was facing up to the fact that the cruise was coming to an end, that this artificial paradise was fading the closer they got to New York. Barbados was the final port, and she described the day in her diary.

Saturday, May 26

> *Up very early to see us come in. Waited about & finally Bill ready & he & his paralytic Mr. Brand & I went ashore in tender. Lovely old place. We took a drive all over the island & ended up at Crane's Hotel. Drink & Bill & I went swimming in terrific surf. We lunched there & had a dance & it was all lovely. Back to ship at 3:30. Drink in Bill's cabin & talked it over. To Mr. Draper's cocktail party. Movies after dinner with Roland & Bill & to Roland's after with them. Perfect day.*

On the following night, after spending as much time as possible all day with Bill, Helen retired to her cabin, "to bed very low that trip so nearly over." Instead of luxuriating in thinking of her homecoming, as she had written her mother, she was realizing that her adventure away from home had run its course.

The *Franconia*'s traditional masquerade dance, held on Monday evening, was called the Raggedy Ann Ball. Passengers were encouraged to wear all their really worn out clothing, including hats and gloves, that were "about to go out of the port hole before the New York arrival." Helen put on a costume but completely lost her enthusiasm and took it off. She just wasn't in the mood for silly fun. Instead, she wrote, "After dinner met Bill & went & lay on #3 hatch & talked. Perfect night. Later to his cabin. Too beautiful & too perfect." How could she bear the end of something this perfect, but the big liner kept cutting through the waves drawing closer to New York. Tuesday was a restless day of goodbye parties. Helen, herself, gave a cocktail party for 45 new friends that she probably would never see again. However, Bill seemed to be in a "queer mood," and she was worried about him. Perhaps he too was feeling low.

Helen, Bill, Roland, and the Van Loons started off the last full day at sea with an early swim in the faux-Greek pool. Packing was followed by more goodbye parties. But suddenly, "a radio [telegram] from Al!! MEETING BOAT MUCH LOVE." A rendezvous with Bill in his cabin later that night turned out to be frustrating as a steady stream of other passengers lingered to say goodbye. "It was too trying & pathetic. I left finally feeling depressed beyond words." Helen's trip was over, the cruise was over, her beautiful evenings with Bill were over. The ship pushed on. She knew there was no stopping it.

Thursday, May 31

To breakfast at Roland's at 6:30. Foghorn bellowing away the minutes & Bill stabbing me every minute with his looks & words. God! On deck later to see all the boats. Champagne with Bill & we said good-by. Forever, I suppose. I should have been so excited getting home & I felt instead as tho my world had fallen to pieces. Docked at 3:30. Al & Marje there, both so sweet. I was the first thru the Customs. To Park Lane for drinks & then had to say good-bye to Marje. Al adorable all the way home. Dinner at Tide Mill Tavern & so bewildered. Home at 10. Mother so sweet & house looking lovely!

Yes, Helen was home, back in Stonington, where everything was familiar. She had been so anxious to leave behind the routine of her life, and now it would resume as before. It was a lovely life filled with family and many friends. But along with all her luggage she brought home albums of memories and complicated feelings, daydreams of a romance that was always going to remain on the *Franconia*. Was anything going to change as a result of her trip? Had she gone halfway around the world only to arrive back where she started from, as though the experience had never happened? One thing seems to be clear. Helen had the self-confidence to accomplish such a venture. She would just need a little time to sort out her mixed emotions before looking into the future.

Friday, June 1

Woke up in my sweet room but feel very odd. I am very definitely feeling the aftermath & now know what Bill meant that a.m. about the spiritual aftermath. I sent him a telegram. Slept after lunch & then Anne came for a while. Harry also came for tea. Al came for dinner, the lamb. He is so understanding & sweet.

Postscript

```
                                    July 29th. 1938

Just got your card.

        Settled here for good.

            A wife,two dogs,a parrot.

                Do not pass us by if visiting.

                    Plenty of room.

Large garden and pool for son(1 foot deep)

    Lost the married name.

        God bless and here's hoping.

                            Bill. Y
```

H elen thought that she had said goodbye to Dr. Carr forever that morning while the *Franconia* was docking in New York. But perhaps not completely. I found this post card among her trip letters. Apparently, Helen had written to Bill, perhaps sent a 1937 photo Christmas card, and here was his cheery reply. They were both married now. Helen had a son, Bill had two dogs and a parrot. He encouraged her to stop by with her little boy but didn't say whether her husband was included or not in that invitation. He had settled in Cannes, France, on the Avenue de la Reine Elizabeth, in a 'villa' called Tahoe.

Indeed, Helen had married Alfred Gildersleeve on March 2, 1935, less than a year after her return from Africa, and their son, Alfred Jr., was born in May of 1936. While her trip had pulled her away from home and opened up a completely new view of the world, it hadn't totally changed her life. She didn't find a handsome diplomat or a colonial settler who was eager to share his idyllic existence with her. And she knew that a shipboard romance would not translate into anything lasting. The place she called home was where she belonged, perhaps with the man who met her at the dock in New York. For his part, Al might have considered that he couldn't risk her going off on an exotic trip again. The story went that when he finally proposed, he made it clear that the marriage had to take place within a couple of weeks or he would lose his nerve. Thus, Helen had to summon her mother and sister back from their Nassau winter vacation in order to be at the March 2nd wedding. And later, whenever the subject of wedding dresses came up, she always stated that she had so little time to prepare that she was married in a navy-blue suit instead of a wedding gown.

Through the births of two more children and a few hurricanes, as well as the home front of the Second World War, Helen's life was more than full. But, in the spring of 1951 she and Al sailed to Europe on the SS *America*. The first stop on their trip was Paris.

*Helen and Alfred Gildersleeve shortly
after their wedding in 1935.*

My Bookshelf and More

I n order to grasp the context of Helen's trip to Africa, I relied on a wide variety of books, references, and articles. And, of course, I'll admit right up front that I didn't hesitate to turn to the internet, especially for basic information on ships, countries, hotels, people, and so on. My Fodor's and Rough Guide on South Africa came in handy, too. Because of my growing interest in Africa, several of these books were already in my own library when I started to write. Many more were added as I went along.

Diamonds, Gold, And War, The British, the Boers, and the Making of South Africa by Martin Meredith (Public Affairs, 2008) is a comprehensive and engrossing history of South Africa and Rhodesia. It covers the life of Cecil Rhodes as well as the background leading to apartheid, taking in events through the 1930s.

The Rhodesia That Was My Life by Sir Robert C. Tredgold, K.C.M.G. (George Allen & Unwin Ltd., 1968) Dedication: *To Lorna, who shared so much of it.*

Other books have influenced and informed my understanding of southern Africa, especially during the 1920s and '30s.

Kenya: *Out of Africa* by Isak Dinesen; *The Bolter* (Idina Sackville) by Frances Osborne; *West with the Night* by Beryl Markham; *Straight on Till Morning* by Mary S. Lovell,

Southern Rhodesia - Zimbabwe: *Under My Skin, Volume One of My Autobiography to 1949* by Doris Lessing; *The Doris Lessing Reader*

(Alfred A. Knopf, 1988); *Don't Let's Go to the Dogs Tonight* and *Cocktail Hour Under the Tree of Forgetfulness*, both by Alexandra Fuller; *Mukiwa, a White Boy in Africa; When a Crocodile Eats the Sun;* and *The Fear, Robert Mugabe and the Martyrdom of Zimbabwe,* all three by Peter Godwin. The blog, Our Rhodesian Heritage, reprinted *The Years Between 1923 – 1973, Half a Century of Responsible Government in Rhodesia* by W.D. Gale, M.B.E. Another blog, bulawayo24.com, offered *Matopos Hills: the other Heroes Acre.*

South Africa: "The Train from Rhodesia" in *The Soft Voice of the Serpent and Other Stories* by Nadine Gordimer; *Conversations with Myself* by Nelson Mandela; "The Nazi Influence in the Formation of Apartheid in South Africa," by Elizabeth Lee Jemison; *South Africa, vol. I* by Anthony Trollope (1877); *Colonial Houses of South Africa* by Graham Viney, photographs by Alain Proust.

For a look at young women in the nineteen-thirties I turned to Frederick Lewis Allen's *Since Yesterday,* a bestselling history of that decade. *A Day at a Time, the diary literature of American women from 1764 to the present,* edited by Margo Culley, helped me understand how much diaries can tell us about their writers. Another book that illuminated Helen's story was *Maiden Voyages, Writing of Women Travelers,* edited by Mary Morris. Morris begins her introduction by pointing to the author John Gardner's statement that "there are only two plots in all of literature. You go on a journey or a stranger comes to town." Women generally waited for that stranger, but *Maiden Voyages* is about those who chose a journey.

The literature on Starr Faithfull is legion, and websites with newspaper accounts abound. In addition to looking at those websites, I acquired an illustrated 300-page book, *The Passing of Starr Faithfull* by Jonathan Goodman (Kent State University Press, 1996) in order to understand this bizarre story. A close-up photo of the drowned young woman's sandy head adorns the book's cover. Even the celebrity Gloria Vanderbilt was transfixed by Starr's sad life and published *The Memory Book of Starr Faithfull, a Novel*, in 1994. Starr's letters to Dr. Carr are the only pieces of non-fiction in the volume.

And last but not least, two books came from Helen's bookshelf. The first is a thick, 600-page tome by Hendrik Van Loon, *The Arts*, published in 1937. It covers the subject from ancient Egypt through the middle of the 20th Century, including ten chapters on music. The book is filled with Van Loon's unique illustrations. The other is a music book, *Folk Songs of Many Lands*, chosen, illustrated and annotated by Van Loon (with Grace Castagnetta) and published in 1938. I remember my mother playing the songs on the piano and singing while we sat next to her.